295

THEOLOGY
AND
PASTORAL
COUNSELING

SUCCESSFUL PASTORAL COUNSELING SERIES

THEOLOGY

AND

PASTORAL

COUNSELING

EDWARD E. THORNTON

PRENTICE-HALL, INC., ENGLEWOOD CLIFFS, N.J.

Theology and Pastoral Counseling
by Edward E. Thornton

© 1964 by Prentice-Hall, Inc., Englewood Cliffs, N.J. All
rights reserved, including the right to reproduce this book or
any portions thereof, in any form, except for the inclusion of
brief quotations in a review.

Library of Congress Catalog Card Number: 64–12847

Printed in the United States of America

T 91326

PRENTICE-HALL INTERNATIONAL, INC., *London*
PRENTICE-HALL OF AUSTRALIA, PTY., LTD., *Sydney*
PRENTICE-HALL OF CANADA, LTD., *Toronto*
PRENTICE-HALL OF FRANCE, S.A.R.L., *Paris*
PRENTICE-HALL OF INDIA (PRIVATE) LTD., *New Delhi*
PRENTICE-HALL OF JAPAN, INC., *Tokyo*
PRENTICE-HALL DE MEXICO, S.A., *Mexico City*

To
Mrs. W. W. Fondren,
who provided the
Fondren Chair of Pastoral Care
in the
Institute of Religion,
Texas Medical Center,
Houston, Texas

ACKNOWLEDGMENTS

In completing this manuscript, I am keenly aware of my debt to Dr. Russell L. Dicks, editor of the series of which this book is a part, for his patience in "breaking in" a new writer—firmly but considerately.

I acknowledge with fraternal affection my debt to Mr. Maurice (Jerry) Ball, Mr. George Thompson, and Mr. Murray Thompson for allowing me to use their verbatim records for clinical illustration. These men have served as theological interns and residents respectively in the ministry of the Institute of Religion to the Texas Medical Center and the Memorial Baptist Hospital of Houston.

Everyone in the field of pastoral theology and counseling knows that his chief teachers are the persons who encounter him in the context of his ministry. Next in importance in the learning process are one's peers in a community of learning and ministry. Also significant are the officially designated "teachers" who have understood one's learning problems and provided colleagueship in learning. Those of my teachers who are in the first two categories must remain nameless here. Fifteen years ago, however, an officially designated "teacher" awakened in me the hope that theology and pastoral counseling may be integrated in my experience, for I found them integrated in him. While I am responsible for the content of these pages, much of the inspiration for writing them and many of the tools employed have been derived from my pilgrimage with this teacher, Wayne E. Oates. I experience distinct joy in acknowledging my debt to him both professionally and personally.

Edward E. Thornton

INTRODUCTION

This series of books represents the most comprehensive publishing effort ever made in the field of pastoral care. These books could not have been published twenty-five years ago, or probably even ten, for the material was not then available. In the past, single books have been available covering different phases of the task. Now we are bringing the subjects together in a single series. Here we present a library of pastoral care covering the major topics and problems that most pastors will encounter in their ministry. Fortunately, not all of these problems need be faced every week or even every month. But, when they are, the minister wants help and he wants it immediately.

These books are prepared for the nonspecialized minister serving the local church, where he is the most accessible professional person in the community. It is a well-accepted fact that more people turn to clergy when in trouble than to all other professional people. Therefore, the pastor must not fail them.

Russell L. Dicks
General Editor

FOREWORD

Edward Thornton brings the skills of a disciplined Christian, an experienced pastor, a patient and thoroughly equipped counselor, and a scholar of theological education in Christian ethics and pastoral care to the book you are about to read. In his exceptionally reflective treatment of theology and pastoral counseling he avoids the old clichés and repetitions that have tended to become the stock and trade of both these areas of intimate interaction within the Christian community. This book is not biased by any sectarian spirit. Nor is it a watered-down version of some particular school of psychotherapy made palatable by use of religious words with no attention to their historical and classical meanings.

Thornton speaks with extraordinary candor about his own pilgrimage as a theologian in the work of the pastor and teacher who has been called to equip the saints for the work of ministry. The case material he uses is appropriate, readable, and demonstrative in more than an anecdotal or wooden way. (Thornton records *his own* in most instances, revealing his failures as well as those instances in which he considers himself to have been effective.)

A fascinating documentary is provided of the coming to maturity-in-experience of a minister *after* he has finished his formal education. Such documents are rare. Therefore, Thornton is too modest when he says that he is speaking to those who have not been extensively schooled in pastoral theology. I have profited by reading these pages and commend the clean differentiation of theological ideas and insights to persons of all branches of theological inquiry. Thornton analyzes competently the data that have been developed in the field of pastoral theology, and builds a significant contribution in his own right. One does get the impression that he is unduly hard on Eduard Thurneysen and possibly has not heard all the

Swiss pastor is trying to say. Also, those active in the clinical pastoral education program of this country may wish that he had made more of the contribution of Daniel Day Williams. The reader senses, however, that the author does not necessarily expect him to agree with his theological positions. Rather, he stimulates the reader to do his own thinking.

Especially helpful to me was the "celebrative" emphasis in pastoral counseling, in which the elements of joy out of suffering and hope out of despair, and the enrichment of the productive life as well as the healing of the chronically or acutely deteriorated life are brought into full expression. This book sets this forth admirably, it seems to me.

Just a personal word can be added. I was privileged to supervise Edward Thornton's doctoral program. As I worked with him as a teacher I received new and exciting insights from him. Reading this book has given me the warm satisfaction of becoming the student of my former student, for I have been taught by him in these pages.

Wayne E. Oates

CONTENTS

CONTENTS

CHAPTER ONE

IS THEOLOGY NEEDED?

Theology and pastoral care interpenetrate each other. Like newlyweds uncertain of one another in the relationship, pastoral counselors and theologians frequently exchange sweet words while anxiously remaining on guard lest the new relationship expose previously concealed weaknesses. This book is written on the assumption that the honeymoon is over and that the time has come for a frank appraisal of both the conflicts and the creative possibilities inherent in the interpenetration of theology and pastoral care.

Some pastors feel that theology is irrelevant to pastoral care and counseling. In pastoral care workshops in which theological discussions occur, a few participants can be counted on to become restless and to walk out or doze off sleepily until the discussion returns to "practical" matters. When asked about this, pastors say that they want practical rather than theoretical instruction. They want to know how *to do* counseling, how *to handle* people who present problems. They feel that counseling is fully acceptable as a method of pastoral work. It does not need to be justified theologically, if it works. People are helped by it, and pastors find fulfillment as counselors, so, they conclude, why become entangled in abstract theological issues?

In the early decades of its development, authorities in pastoral counseling fostered the separation of theology and counseling. Occasionally, exponents of the "new" counseling approach to ministry and of the "old" homiletical, theological approach impugned each other's motives. At best, pastoral counseling was interpreted as an *application* of theology, without mention of its contribution toward the *apprehension* of theology. It was defended theologically on the ground that it *communicates* the faith. Its role as a *critic, corrector* and *illuminator* of the faith was ignored. Inevitably, pastoral counseling soon came to be thought of as a "how to do it" field of study.

Since World War II, we have started seriously to ask what pastoral counseling has to contribute to the "why" of theological inquiry.

To suggest that a pastoral function, such as counseling, can contribute substantially to our understanding of the faith throws some ministers into a panic. They fear that theology is in danger of being perverted. Case analyses from a theological perspective can only contaminate theology and confuse the course of one's counseling ministry. Theological ideas are derived from revelation and not from empirical inquiry. The faith is not subject, therefore, to examination —and certainly not to change—on the basis of human experience. No dialogue between theology and pastoral counseling is thereby possible.

I do not share either of these opposing views. Both positions say in effect that theology is not needed in pastoral counseling; they imply that theology and pastoral care do not interpenetrate each other. My experience has led me to the position that theology is decisive in trying to answer the questions that emerge from counseling. On the other side, reflection upon my experience with people in crises stimulates, corrects and illuminates my understanding of the faith. Counseling serves me at the point of both application and apprehension of theology. In fact, my theology *is* my theory of pastoral care and counseling, and reflection on pastoral functioning constitutes an important methodological aspect of my theological thinking.

The purpose of this book is to define the central purpose of pastoral care and counseling in terms of pastoral theology. I make no claim to originality. "Veterans" in pastoral theology have already established a beachhead and mapped out a strategy. My intention is to speak to front-line clergymen and to those who have not been extensively schooled in pastoral theology. I propose to share my understanding of the theological questions which need to be asked and the answers which are emerging at this point. The most honest kind of introduction for a work of this kind seems to me to be a review of my own pastoral experience from the standpoint of my discovery that theology is decisive in pastoral work. The remainder of the chapter traces, in long steps and broad jumps, experiences that have shaped the point of view to be presented in the following chapters.

After one year in a student pastorate, I was overjoyed because a young woman told the church of her decision to enter a church-related vocation. She felt called to become a missionary. I was a bachelor minister only a few years older than she. We enjoyed each other's company in the context of church work. I was frequently in her home on the invitation of her parents, but I remained highly circumspect in relation to her—always being the minister, never the friend or companion.

My view of the role of the minister at that time could be categorized as "the suffering servant." I felt that a pastor should set an example of piety and moral purity even if such behavior cloaked him in artificiality. The last thing I wanted to be was myself. If, as I suspected, my self really contained some hostile, erotic or irresponsible impulses, I felt compelled to conceal these feelings. The best method of doing so was to saturate my conscious mind in pious thoughts, fill my speech with spiritual words and drive myself relentlessly in the performance of good deeds for the glory of God. I felt sure in my private thoughts that the young lady was fortunate to have so "spiritual" a young pastor as I to emulate. She would, I was confident, develop into a dedicated religious worker.

Two years later she left the community—pregnant out of wedlock. Several months earlier she had withdrawn from leadership in youth activities. I had heard that her courtship with a young man who was not in our church was less than consistent with my Pietistic ideals. I was not prepared, however, for what happened.

My initial response was one of anger. I asked: Who sinned? And I answered: Not only this girl and boy, but also the parents and adults who worked with them in Sunday school and in public school. I had become comfortably settled in my self-righteous indignation against all of these other people when some of the ladies of the church said in my hearing, "Of course, you know she had a crush on the preacher." "Yes," another said, "I think she started to run around when she realized that the preacher was not going to notice her."

I was devastated. Could this be? Did I share responsibility for her defiant behavior? Can a man share in sin when he is personally pious and above reproach?

This pastoral experience disclosed for me large needs for self-discovery and maturation which I shall not elaborate on here. It disclosed, also, an inadequate doctrine of sin. I was launched as a pastoral theologian from this point. For I began to ask with new seriousness: What is sin? It became quite clear that sin was more fundamentally related to motivations and attitudes than to behavior. But, I had assumed that sin was individually defined. At this point, I began to question whether we are not all involved in the sins of one another? If so, who then is righteous? I began also to take a fresh look at my motives in this relationship. Here in the congregation had been an admiring young lady to whom I had given nothing of myself. In this sense, I, too, had exploited her. I had not really heard her nor had I responded to her in a genuinely human way. My pious aloofness and my inhibiting purity had spun one strand of the web in which several people had been caught and seriously hurt.

Soon thereafter I found that I was not the first person to discover the tragic dimension of life. In an introductory course in systematic theology, I vibrated wholeheartedly to the doctrines of the universality of sin and the tragic bondage of man (which is pointed to in the concept of original sin), because they plucked my experience in pastoral relationships. I began to preach repeatedly on texts such as Romans 3:10 and 23: "There is none righteous, no, not one. . . . For all have sinned, and come short of the glory of God."[1] With razor-like incisions, I defined for my parishioners the sin of feeling one's self above sinning, the sin of seeking to safeguard one's self from sin and guilt, the futility of pious thoughts, words and acts in the service of such goals as these. At this point, I knew more about sin than about grace, but I had at least assimilated one lesson in theology. It was a lesson which, emerging from pastoral functioning, effectively modified some of my previous theology.

A few years later, as a seminarian, I provided pastoral care to a member of my church who suffered an emotional illness. This man was about 35 years old, a laborer, father of three children and a nominal church member. He became depressed and was hospitalized in a hospital where I was employed as a psychiatric aide. Because of my dual relation to him as psychiatric aide and pastor, we quickly developed deep bonds of concern and respect. He left the hospital against medical advice, however. With the approval of the medical staff, I continued to see him in a counseling relationship during my week-end visits to my pastorate. A critical incident occurred a few

[1] All scriptural references are quoted from the Revised Standard Version of the Holy Bible, Copyright 1946, 1952, by the Division of Christian Education, National Council of Churches.

weeks later. He voiced despair over his lack of progress, and I felt compelled to offer him some reassurance. Distorting psychiatric information that I had picked up in the hospital, I assured him authoritatively that he could not expect marked improvement for at least a year from the onset of his depression. By implication, I told him that in a year he could expect improvement.

Exactly one year from the onset of his illness, he committed suicide. The medical community in which he had been a patient and in which I was employed afforded me a ministry in my despair— without resorting to authoritative pronouncements, incidentally. I cannot be certain that my false prediction of improved health had anything to do with his suicide, but I was deeply enough involved with him to say that his suicide represented hostility evoked in part by me or by his unrealistic expectation of help from me—an expectation which I did little to modify.

At this point in my pilgrimage I had participated in tragic consequences related to pious aloofness and to pastoral involvement. I was not totally unaware of the unconscious dimensions of life but was not fully convinced that psychiatric understandings of man were valid. What had gone wrong? What did this experience have to teach me about pastoral ministry?

My theological education in this experience focused on the doctrine of man. Previously, my understanding of behavior consisted of religious lore decorated with a bit of psychiatric information. Fundamentally, I had not assimilated the basic contribution of all psychiatric theories of personality into my own view of man. I did not fully accept the reality and power of unconscious mental processes in the motivation of behavior.

Paradoxically, my pastoral counseling had been determined by an exaggerated need to reassure the man that he would be mentally well again. At this point, I was more concerned to serve the psychiatric goal of mental health than the theological goal of spiritual growth in the midst of mental illness. This experience forced me to re-examine my theology of suffering as well as my psychological need to be reassuring. I asked myself: What is the purpose of pastoral counseling? Is it to allay the suffering of mental illness in the service of the goals of health? Or is it to allay the suffering which arises from loss of meaning in the face of illness? Is it to serve health, medically defined, or to inspire hope, theologically defined? If the pastoral goal is the recovery of faith in the midst of suffering, of what value are psychiatric understandings of man?

Suicide meant a sure judgment of eternal damnation in the thinking of some members of the congregation. I was enlightened by psychiatry, however. I knew—and said—that suicide is the result of sickness, not of sin. But, privately, I began to wonder how one discriminates between sickness and sin. This man had undergone a renewal of his religious commitments during the course of his illness. Why, then, was he denied emotional health? Is there not health potential in salvation? If there was an element of sin in the man's act of suicide, could it have been in his prior act of "rededication" to God? Could this have been a kind of bargaining with God? If so, then suicide would be a man's logical response to God's obvious failure to deliver him from his depression.

Once again, a pastoral experience became my schoolmaster in theology. If the task of a successful teacher is to awaken in a student important questions, my congregation was rapidly qualifying for the chairmanship of a department of theology.

At this point I wish to break the chronology of my experience to present a counseling relationship of more recent date. It illustrates a garden-variety kind of problem appearing in the context of a pastor's routine appointments. If counseling and theology belong together, the relationship needs to be demonstrated in usual as well as in unusual experiences.

A young woman of 25, a college graduate employed as a secretary, came to me for guidance in finding God's will concerning her engagement and prospective marriage. Since college days she and a young man had a private understanding that they were "in love" and would get married sometime. Though they lived in separate towns following graduation, he pressed for an early wedding date. Each time they set a date for the wedding, she felt herself "torn apart" and "in a panic." The date had been postponed twice on this account, and at the time of our conversation no date was set. The first time he visited her after pressing her to set a date, she began to feel anger toward him. She also felt extremely guilty about some limited petting. She decided to seek counseling after a second visit from the young man, during which they had talked again about setting a new wedding date and had indulged in heavy petting. She had experienced acute anxiety and panic during the entire period of her fiancé's visit.

Subsequently, she lost considerable weight. Medical examination failed to locate the cause of her weight loss. Her internist called in a psychiatrist for consultation, but she refused to talk with him. Instead, she came to a pastoral counselor, feeling that her basic problem was to know and do "the Lord's will" in this matter.

Both of these young people had felt for some time that their plan to marry was "the Lord's will." After she began to feel herself in conflict about her fiancé, she felt that God was speaking to her "through conscience," telling her not to marry him. He, however, continued to feel certain that their contemplated marriage was "the Lord's will." He was willing to wait. She respected him as a good Christian, and since he was so sure their marriage was in God's will, she did not feel confident in trusting the message of her conscience. She said that her conscience punished her severely for what she regarded as extremely intense sexual desires. She felt that a good Christian should be able to control sexual feelings and enjoy limited physical contact—such as kissing—without being overwhelmed with a desire for intercourse. She also felt disturbed that one seriously seeking to know and do God's will should experience such intense conflict over what to do about marriage.

She told me that she knew her past experiences in her family had much to do with her present problem. After reviewing her family situation, I agreed. She did not feel, however, that she could talk to a psychiatrist, for she thought he would not understand her religious feelings. Most of all, she wanted to do the Lord's will. In her teens she had believed she should be a missionary. These feelings had recently returned with new force. If I could assure her that a psychiatrist was a good Christian, she said, she might risk talking with him, but she would prefer talking to a minister.

My immediate problem was to decide whether to enter into pastoral counseling with her or to refer her to a psychiatrist. The question requires some psychological as well as theological answers. I decided to refer her and succeeded in making the referral for intensive psychotherapy.

Left unanswered, however, are at least two theological questions: (1) How does spiritual growth occur? What is the process of change, not only at the level of sexual identity and emotional freedom for entering into marriage, but also at the level of discerning the will of God and making decisions in faith without the presence of any kind of guarantee? Does spiritual growth require psychological growth and change? What does this young woman's hunger to know the will of God mean? What does this say about her spiritual condition? (2) What is the theological basis for referral to a psychiatrist in cases involving problems of conscience? Do not the needs of this young woman fall clearly within the area of the church's ministry of healing and of guidance? If a pastor refers persons like her, does he not abdicate an area of pastoral responsibility that is traditionally his? On what grounds should a psychiatrist be trusted with a young woman's struggle to know the will of God?

As I reflect further upon these questions, I become quickly immersed in the need to discriminate between sick and healthy manifestations of religious behavior. This raises questions about the meaning of the "demonic" in religious experience. The nature of ministry and the meaning of ordination come into question in relation to the resources of the psychiatrist. These questions drive one back to the nature and purpose of the church and the relation of health to salvation.

The purpose of this illustration, like the purpose of this book, is not to presume to answer all of these difficult questions. It *is* to demonstrate that pastoral counseling raises questions that require theological answers and that theology is enhanced when it is subject to the scrutiny of these same questions.

The doctrines of church and ministry became central for me after about a year as an associate pastor of a large, downtown church. I had been called by the congregation to provide a specialized ministry in the area of pastoral care and counseling. The membership included nearly a thousand persons who were totally nonparticipant in the life of the church; many of them were unknown to the members who participated. More than four hundred were in the geriatric phase of life—65 years of age or older. One hundred of these were shut-ins. Young people included many college, nursing and other student groups who made heavy demands for vocational and premarital counseling. Single adults living in downtown apartments were numerous. Their calls for counseling were not frequent, but their needs were great, and counseling was usually time-consuming, once begun. Approximately seven hundred units of government housing adjacent to the church property afforded a concentration of persons, most of whom were living on the brink of disintegration financially, emotionally and often maritally. The adults who provided the core of leadership and financial support for the church were oppressed by the usual demands of successful middle-class persons. On almost any single day from one to a dozen parishioners were admitted to local hospitals scattered over a metropolitan area 20 miles in length. In a typical month I was consulted by parishioners on problems which included marital disintegration, mental illness, retardation, delinquency, poverty and bereavement. Consultations focusing on problems of intrachurch factionalism increased as members reacted anxiously to changes in policy and personnel initiated by the senior pastor.

To this task I brought the concept that the ordained minister is the shepherd of the flock. With a Bachelor of Divinity degree and considerable clinical pastoral training, I felt qualified to deal with the persons in crises who came to my attention. After several months, however, the size of the task began to overwhelm me. I realized that while my ministry was meaningful to those with whom I spent major amounts of time and energy, I was tending more and more to go through the motions of ministry under a sense of compulsion to extend the ministry of the church to all who needed it. It soon became clear that I must make a decision. Either I must limit ministry to a few persons and make sure that they received a qualitatively meaningful service or I must run on the treadmill of comprehensive "coverage" and be significantly related to few, if any, of the people involved.

Neither alternative was satisfactory. Finally, a third alternative appeared. Readings in the New Testament awakened in me the idea that the church itself ought to be the shepherd. (This was before H. Richard Niebuhr defined the image of "pastoral director" and before the concept of the lay ministry had reached me in published form.) I began to ask how my time could be invested in such a way as to implement the ideal concept of lay shepherding. In conversation with the senior pastor and others, a plan (later published) was devised.[2] This program of lay shepherding was not unique. It was from an original moment of theological thinking for me that the plan emerged, however. The questions posed by an overwhelming pastoral task caused the church to try to solve them by employing another staff member. The same problems prodded me to try to

[2] Edward E. Thornton, "These Deacons Led Out," *Church Administration*, I, No. 3 (December, 1959), pp. 34–35.

solve them by asking what the theological meaning of shepherding is or ought to be.

During the next year much of my time was devoted to the supervision of laymen as they carried out their shepherding functions. Classes in "The Art of Ministering to the Sick" were formed, using Russell Dicks' *You Came Unto Me*[3] as a textbook. Supervision of actual visitation was a popular and productive aspect of the class experience.

As I shifted from individual counseling to the supervision of lay groups, I began to see the potential of Sunday school groups in implementing the shepherding goals of the church. Adults in the church were agitated at the time because familiar patterns in the Sunday school were being broken up in favor of smaller groups. The denominational "party line" lifted up the goal of evangelism and numerical growth as the primary justification for smaller groups. Class members resisted the changes because they prized their experiences of social support and of "togetherness" in the old, familiar, overgrown classes.

The growing pains related to these changes demanded that the ministerial leadership of the church go back to the theology of the church for a reliable perspective. Togetherness in the early church was called *koinonia*. *Koinonia* then meant something quite different from present-day togetherness. The early church lived and grew in small groups, but it was not primarily concerned with "a million more in A.D. '54."[4] These small groups were deeply concerned with discipline, mutual confession and the experience of forgiveness. They were committed to the use of prayers and anointings for the sick. These ministries were performed by lay "elders" of the church. The small-group structure of the early church appeared primarily to comprise shepherding groups. The questions which emerged from problems of educational administration evoked new apprehension of the theology of the church. When this theology is brought into contact with the existential problems of a twentieth-century Sunday school, some of these problems take on a new appearance and the nature of

[3] Russell L. Dicks, *You Came Unto Me: A Guidebook in Pastoral Calling for Ministers and Laymen,* now revised under the title, *How To Make Pastoral Calls* (St. Louis: The Bethany Press, 1962).

[4] My denomination was engaged in a campaign of Sunday school enlargement under the slogan, "A Million More in '54" at the time of this experience.

the problem changes. Once again, the interdependence of pastoral functions and theology becomes clear.

I have alluded to growing factionalism in the church. By job description as well as by disposition I was not involved in the administrative life of the church. As a minister of pastoral care, I quickly endeared myself to many members and avoided most of the hostility which other staff members received. I maneuvered into the role of an apostle of love—a suffering servant for the people. I was safe from the hostile impulses being fired all around. I was safe but unhappy. It was clearly apparent that my ministry of loving pastoral care did nothing to heal the raw wounds of strife within the congregation. It was equally clear that had I been in the seat of administrative authority, I could not have functioned by the criterion of love alone. Judgment and justice were needed as well as love.

The conclusion of this episode was reached when, within two months of each other, both the senior pastor and I resigned. The conflict within the church membership was inflamed even more by our resignations than it had been by our leadership. It was not until several years later that I found in Tillich's discussion of *Love, Power and Justice* a theological answer to this pastoral problem.[5] But the way was prepared for just this theological lesson by living through a major church controversy. Had the theology been assimilated by the pastoral staff at the time of the controversy, it might have provided the perspective which we needed to deal more creatively with the situation than we did.

The critical incidents which I have reviewed here, as well as many others which I omitted, have prodded me to the conclusion that pastoral care and theology interpenetrate each other. Theirs is not a contradictory or complementary mode of relationship, nor a parallel or paradoxical one. They interpenetrate. Each inheres in the other. Tension and contrast mark their relationship, but not separation and contradiction. Pastoral functions and theological interpretations are not antagonistic to each other, nor are they assimilated into each other. They exist in correlation. Theology and pastoral care maintain commerce with each other on a two-way street. It is impossible always to tell in which lane one travels from theology to

[5] Paul Tillich, *Love, Power and Justice* (Gloucester, Mass.: Peter Smith, 1960), (New York: Oxford University Press, 1954).

pastoral care and in which lane one makes the return trip. But significant interchange regularly occurs.

The study of the interpenetration of theology and pastoral care (including counseling) has emerged today as pastoral theology. For many of us pastoral theology was born in the painful question: Who am I—as a minister? It continues to take form in the question: Who is God in relation to human existence? Another way of tracing the emergence of contemporary pastoral theology in the experience of many pastors is to say that one is pledged to the pastoral theology fraternity when he asks how to communicate the gospel. He is actually initiated when he goes on to ask: What is the gospel itself? What is the nature of the relationship between the gospel and our methods of communicating it?

Pastoral theology emerges in the context of ministry when one listens to his doubt and his perplexity as well as to his faith and certainty; it is stimulated by attention to one's successes as well as to one's failures. Pastoral theology is a discipline sustained by the hope that the concrete realities of pastoral ministry will contribute to a valid synthesis of what now appear to be fragmentary and occasionally contradictory forms of both theology and pastoral care.

CHAPTER TWO

PREPARE The WAY For SALVATION

We now shift our focus from the clinical situations from which theological conversations emerge to the theological statements with which clinical work is both informed and re-formed. I begin with a definition of the purpose of pastoral care and counseling and move to a statement of faith. *Pastoral care and counseling are forms of religious ministry which integrate the findings of behavioral science and theology in the effort to prepare the way for divine-human encounter in the midst of human crises.*

Any statement about the purpose of pastoral counseling presupposes a statement of faith. This is true because the purpose of a pastoral function cannot be defined theologically apart from the purpose of the church and of ministry in all its forms. The purpose of the church and of ministry presupposes a theological understanding of the purpose of God in the world. And a statement about the purpose of God in the world is an affirmation of faith. In order to offer a theological viewpoint concerning the purpose of pastoral care and counseling, I must begin with a statement of faith and work back to the proposition stated above.

What is God's intention toward us? *God intends to meet us with salvation in every experience of life!* This intention is present in the threat of destruction as well as in the promise of deliverance. Isaiah articulated this faith when he warned Ahaz of impending doom as a result of the king's alliance with Assyria. The prophetic sign of destruction was not the desertion of Israel by her Lord; the promised sign was the birth of a son named Immanuel: God is with us (Isaiah 7:14, 8:8). God is immanent in an event of judgment. The New Testament ascription of the name Immanuel to Jesus (Matthew 1:23) affirms that God is immanent in a decisive event of deliverance.

In the face of the Babylonian exile, the prophet known as Deutero-

Isaiah perceived a new meaning in the tragic events of his time. He saw the suffering of the Jewish remnant not merely as a punishment for idolatry; he saw the remnant as a servant of God suffering vicariously in order to be given as a light to the Gentiles. The restoration and preservation of Israel seemed assured to the prophet for one purpose primarily: "that thou mayest be my salvation unto the end of the earth" (Isaiah 49:6). The servant of God who would accomplish God's encounter of man and who in doing so would bring man salvation could be expected to travel incognito. He would appear in obscure and repulsive form; he would be despised and rejected of men. But he would effectively encounter men nonetheless.

> Surely he has borne our griefs and carried our sorrows; yet we esteemed him stricken, smitten by God, and afflicted. But he was wounded for our transgressions, he was bruised for our iniquities; upon him was the chastisement that made us whole, and with his stripes we are healed. All we like sheep have gone astray; we have turned every one to his own way; and the Lord has laid on him the iniquity of us all (Isaiah 53:4–6).

This anticipation is realized in Jesus of Nazareth. In Jesus, God is disclosed to us; he is perceived to be among us. He is disclosed in the babe of Bethlehem. In faith, he is seen to be the incarnation of the eternal Word. The Word was not thundered at man; it was not engraved with fire on mountain cliffs. "The Word became flesh, and dwelt among us" (John 1:14). In Jesus Christ, God is perceived to be among us. He is among us not only in worship (Matthew 18:20) but also in the person of those who hunger and thirst, those who are strangers and who go naked in the world—inadequately protected from the elements, and those who are sick and in prison (Matthew 25:35–36). God's purpose is to meet us in every experience of life. The possibility of divine-human encounter is particularly real in the crisis experiences of life.

Every human experience is potentially revelatory. The ground of meeting between God and men is not fenced by ecclesiastical or dogmatic barriers; it is not prescribed by sex, race, class or nation; the prerequisite for divine-human encounter is neither a particular psychological disposition nor a state of emotional and physical health. Consciousness and rationality are not the sole grounds for this decisive encounter.

God meets us today as he met the Biblical writers and their contemporaries—in Jesus Christ, who is the incarnation of the Word.
God meets us in our hope of his appearing. He meets us in our
memory of his having appeared. He encounters us in our perception
of his having always been and his continuing to be in the world.
The Christian community understands itself to be *the* continuing
incarnation of God in the world. Pastoral care, as one form of Christian ministry, participates in the continuing incarnation. In this
sense, pastoral care may prepare the way for divine-human encounter
in the midst of crisis experiences.

But is it not contradictory for us to say that the ground of meeting
between God and man is not fenced and then to say that God meets
us in Jesus Christ—in the continuing incarnation of Christ in the
church? A contradiction exists if we think of the church exclusively
in terms of formal, religious affiliation and if we think of the church
only as it is gathered for worship and instruction. If we think also of
the church dispersed in the world, serving the world in the name of
Jesus Christ, we may perceive Christ in the most unlikely places—
meaning the most irreligious communities and the most ordinary
experiences. The parable of the sheep and goats (Matthew 25:31–
46) teaches us that some men will discover that unbeknown to
themselves they have been on God's side all along. Unaffiliated with
the institutional church and perhaps opposed by religious zealots,
their commitment to Christ is known by their participation in the
purpose of God in the world. They respond unconsciously to the
vicarious suffering of God-in-Christ by participating in his suffering
in behalf of those who hunger and thirst, who are strangers and
naked, who are sick and in prison. I shall discuss the role of unconscious mental processes more explicitly in relation to repentance,
faith and commitment.

God's intention is to meet us not only in emotional health but also
in mental illness. For thousands of years mental illness was understood to be a form of demon possession. Then in 1920 a minister
named Anton Boisen suffered a mental illness. Four years later,
Boisen became a full-time Protestant chaplain in a mental hospital.
He, more than any other person, has awakened us to God's intention
to meet men in mental illness as well as in mental health. Boisen
understands his own illness as a religious experience. At stake were
issues of spiritual life and death. While still a patient, he saw that

the functional psychoses of many patients around him were mani-festations of religious as well as of medical problems. Mental illness is one's response to the disorganization of one's inner world. A death, an acute disappointment or a pervasive sense of failure may trigger the disorganization. The illness becomes a way both of denying or concealing one's feelings and of confessing them and crying for understanding and help. One may withdraw, drift or fight in re-sponse to the disorganization of one's inner world. But God's inten-tion is to meet, sustain and deliver the sufferer from his isolation and disintegration. If demons are involved in mental illness, we ought not to speak of demon possession but of demons *being engaged by God* in the life of an individual.

As recently as 1935, Boisen could write with accuracy that

> if a man has a broken leg he can in almost any part of the country be cared for in a church hospital, at church expense, and under church auspices; but if he has a broken heart he is sent to a state institution, there to be forgotten by the church.[1]

By 1960, however, the Association of Mental Hospital Chaplains numbered more than 300 in its membership. These chaplains—Catholics, Protestants and Jews—witness to a growing conviction in both religious and medical communities that God's intention is to meet men in the midst of mental illness.

God's intention is to meet us not only in consciousness but also in our unconscious mental processes. Specifically, God meets us in our dreams. Jacob fled from his enraged brother, Esau, and in sleep "he dreamed . . . and Jacob awoke from his sleep, and said, Surely the Lord is in this place; and I did not know it" (Genesis 28:12, 16). Had Jacob understood God's intention in a way characteristic of many modern believers—including most ministers—he would have rubbed his head and muttered about the wild dreams which dis-turbed his sleep. Then he would have pulled himself together to face the rigors of the day ahead without giving his dream life serious thought.

Jacob, in contrast to moderns, was attentive to God's visitation in dreams and in sleepless nights. I can imagine a modern minister

[1] Anton T. Boisen, *The Exploration of the Inner World: A Study of Mental Disorder and Religious Experience* (New York: Willett, Clark and Company, 1936), p. 222.

reacting to a sleepless night preceding a crucial meeting by reaching for a sedative, rationalizing that he needs to be refreshed for his big day on the morrow. He might supply himself with tranquilizers. But Jacob allowed God to engage him at the depths of his being during the sleepless night prior to his reunion with Esau. From this encounter Jacob emerged with a new identity. The change in him was symbolized by a new name, Israel: "for you have striven with God and with men and have prevailed. . . . So Jacob called the name of the place Peniel, saying, For I have seen God face to face, and yet my life is preserved" (Genesis 32:28, 30).

Matthew perceived Joseph, the father of our Lord, to be a man who was attentive to God's encounter in dreams. He writes that "an angel of the Lord appeared to Joseph in a dream and said, Rise, take the child and his mother, and flee to Egypt. . . . And he rose and took the child and his mother by night, and departed to Egypt" (Matthew 2:13–14). Is it conceivable that the life of Jesus might have been lost if Joseph had regarded his dream life as out of bounds so far as God's self-disclosure is concerned?

God's intention is to meet man not in isolation but in the context of a community of faith. It was in the context of a community of faith that the men just mentioned found meaning to their dreams. The uniqueness of the Hebrew-Christian understanding of God inheres in the particularity and concreteness of the community in which God discloses himself. Jesus Christ chose to limit his immediate ministry "to the lost sheep of the house of Israel" (Matthew 10:6). God, the Holy Spirit, disclosed himself at Pentecost not to individuals in isolation from one another but to persons identified with the church as the corporate Body of Christ. The role of a community of faith will be discussed at length in a subsequent chapter, but it deserves mention here. *The theme of divine-human encounter is to be understood throughout this discussion as a reference to encounter within community not in isolation from one's community of faith.*

In the ministry of Jesus we discern God's intention to meet us in the midst of illnesses and physical handicaps of all kinds. In Mark 7:31–37 Jesus is shown healing a speech impediment and deafness. In Mark 8:22–26 he healed blindness. In both instances he used spittle in connection with a word of command. The Fourth Gospel records the healing of a man born blind by the application of spittle to clay and the anointing of the eyes with the clay (John 9:1–7). The healing value of saliva was widely affirmed in the ancient world. In Mark 5:1–20 Jesus is shown as an exorcist casting the demons out of the so-called Gerasene Demoniac. Mark does not imply that Jesus questioned the demonology which prevailed in medical psychology at the time. He tells the story to show that Jesus is the Son of God and that the Son of God meets man at the point of total isolation and hopeless disorganization and leaves him "clothed and in his right mind" (Mark 5:15).

These passages have been cited because they show Jesus affirming the medical procedures that were generally regarded as beneficial. Without contradicting or devaluing these medical procedures, Jesus transcended them. What is remarkable about the Biblical witness to Jesus' ministry of healing is not in his methods but in his results. His methods and, by implication, his theoretical understanding of the physiology and psychology of disease were linked inextricably with the medical and psychological theories of the time. What is distinctive about his healing ministry is the dramatic power of his person. To modern men the central challenge of Jesus' ministry of healing is the challenge to prepare the way for his continuing encounter of men in the midst of illness, handicap and tragedy.

God's intention to meet man with both healing and salvation is dramatically told in John 9. The Fourth Gospel records this event as a sign of Jesus' identity as the incarnate Word. Central to the meaning of incarnation is the discussion by Jesus and his disciples of the meaning of blindness to a man, born blind, who sat and begged. The disciples asked Jesus to disclose the cause of his blindness. Was it caused by his sin or the sin of his parents? Jesus said, in effect, the meaning of his blindness (and of all human crises) is not to be found in seeking its cause. The meaning is to be found in an encounter between the sufferer and the incarnate Word who is potentially present in every experience. Jesus was seen by his followers to be the light of the world to the blind, the water and bread of life to the thirsty and hungry, the resurrection to the dying.

To be met by God-in-Christ is to be made whole. The man born blind received his sight from Jesus—only to be excommunicated by the Pharisees. The Gospel concludes the account with a second encounter between the man and Jesus. In this meeting, Jesus disclosed his identity as "the Son of Man" and the man said, "Lord, I believe;

and he worshipped him" (John 9:35, 38). Then an ironic shift occurs. An episode which began with Jesus' healing the blindness of a beggar ends with Jesus despairing in the face of the Pharisees' refusal to be healed of their blindness. Theirs was the blindness of believing themselves not blind. They would not see that God intended to meet them in his incarnate son; they were blind to God's self-disclosure in Jesus' healing of a beggar. God's intention through incarnation is to meet man with healing as a sign of salvation and to meet man with salvation as the ultimate in health.

A pastor's personal life and his public ministry are filled with contemporary evidence of God's continuing intention to meet man with health and salvation. Frequently the pastor who is crippled by an involutional depression or by heart disease regrets not having followed his physician's recommendation to build more recreation into his life and to pace himself in a way appropriate to his human limitations. I have in mind several ministers who interpreted this kind of advice from physicians as the devil's counsel. Subsequently some of these men decided that God, not the devil, was seeking to engage them in conversation through the mouths of physicians. They have discovered that the inability to pace themselves was due to neurotic bondage as much as to divine directive.

Others have refused to see and hear God in their illness and in their doctor's advice. The wife of a wealthy patient suffering with an ulcer told me in the flat voice of apathy that at the time of marriage her husband told her he would turn from money making to enjoying human relations when he had ten thousand dollars in reserve. When he had ten thousand he had to have one hundred thousand; when he had one hundred thousand he had to have a million. He had long since passed the million mark. Still he did not have time for people. He was then undergoing surgical repair of ulcers—a procedure which had been repeated many times already. His prognosis was poor. His wife reported that doctor after doctor had told him he must change his style of life if he wished to be well. He had changed doctors instead. The chaplain was not a welcome visitor at this time, either.

In relation to this family, I saw clearly that God may speak to one who is ill through the voice of his physician as surely as through the voice of a minister or any other means. I saw, too, that ultimately the struggle is not at the level of the encounter between doctor and patient or pastor and parishioner but that the encounter is between Creator and creature. This is real, of course, only to eyes of faith, but in the context of faith this perception of God's intention defines the pastor's purpose in ministry.

We may return now to the proposition set forth in the opening paragraph of this chapter. The purpose of pastoral care and counseling is *to prepare the way for divine-human encounter* in the midst of human crises. What is the content of divine-human encounter? Toward what does this language point? The content of divine-human encounter is the forgiveness of sins, the experience of grace. It is salvation and sanctification conceived of as inseparable aspects of a continuing experience. It is man's discovery that he exists before God and that God, who once was feared, may now be freely trusted and loved. The apostle Paul speaks of being "justified by faith" (Romans 5:1) and of being "reconciled" to God; he defines Christian ministry as the ministry "of reconciliation" (2 Corinthians 5:19–20). Paul Tillich speaks of the courage to accept acceptance.[2] Eduard Thurneyson says, "*the* question with which pastoral care is concerned is this: 'Do you know that all your sins are forgiven you in Jesus Christ?'"[3]

The early church understood Jesus to be concerned primarily with the forgiveness of sins. On a few occasions in his healing ministry he dramatically made the content of his interpersonal relationships explicit by saying to the person under his care, "your sins are forgiven" (Mark 2:5; cf. Matthew 9:2 and Luke 5:20). The theme of forgiveness occurs specifically more often in his preaching and in his teaching than in his healing ministry, however.

To define the content of divine-human encounter as the communication of grace or the forgiveness of sin is one thing. To prepare the way for such an encounter is quite another matter. To know the ultimate word in theological terms does not equip one to communicate it effectively in existential relationships. The purpose of pastoral care and counseling is only superficially defined if we ignore the clinical realities toward which the theological statement points. The preparation of the way for the communication of divine grace is an

[2] Paul Tillich, *The Courage To Be* (New Haven: Yale University Press, 1962), p. 155.

[3] Eduard Thurneysen, *A Theology of Pastoral Care* (Richmond, Va.: John Knox Press, 1962), p. 154.

extremely complex task deserving the utmost in professional competence and religious commitment.

The complexity of the task inheres in the nature of man—in what may be described theologically as man's struggle against grace. In general hospital ministry I am impressed by the tenacious way many patients hold that the meaning of their illness is a punishment for sins. Initially, I felt that this interpretation of illness was due to faulty religious education prior to the onset of illness. Now it appears to me that these patients reflect a universal human tendency to avoid the anxiety of feeling helpless in the hands of what seems to be an impersonal, irrational fate. Affirming that I am ill with cancer because God is punishing me for my sins is a more tolerable, ego-satisfying interpretation than concluding that I am victim of a disease process which is indifferent to my personal identity. My personal identity is clearly defined by my sins. Often a person can more easily tell who he essentially is by reciting his sins than by reciting his virtues. To accept grace means to stand not on my merits, but on the merits of another who is gracious toward me. The danger of losing my personal identity and my feeling of self-esteem is implicit in an offer of grace. To cope with my sense of guilt by some kind of self-achieved atonement makes me feel adequate in one respect at least. It makes me feel adequate in handling my feelings of inadequacy. So I cling to the view that my suffering is a punishment for my sins. In suffering I feel that I am adequately solving the problem of guilt. My self-esteem is salved to some extent. I am reassured that I exist as an individual of consequence. God has taken special notice of me by punishing me. I am not being rewarded in accord with my deserts, but at least I am not ignored.

How does one communicate the Word of grace to a person who clings to the feeling that his illness is a punishment for sins? Reading the Scriptures, reasoning about one's theology and even prayer fail to modify the attitudes of most patients. The pastor's dilemma is that his words are not effective in communicating the divine Word. Even reciting the Scriptures fails to effectively communicate the Word of forgiveness and reconciliation. We are in much the same position as the psychiatrist who in a cartoon was portrayed standing over an agitated patient shouting, "Relax! Relax!! Relax!!!" How does a psychiatrist effectively communicate to his patient the feeling of relaxation? How does a minister effectively communicate to his parishioner the feeling "God loves me—I am loved!"

This is our dilemma. We have not defined the purpose of pastoral care and counseling until we have defined both the content of divine-human encounter and the process by which a pastor prepares the way for this decisive encounter. Perhaps, then, deeds will communicate where words fail.

While chaplain of a home for dependent and delinquent children, I observed the failure of deeds to overcome entrenched resistance against grace. A cottage of 12-year-old boys had been assigned a Methodist men's group as sponsors. These men were more active and more genuinely interested in the boys than were sponsors of any other cottage on the campus. They planned a rapid round of ball games, trips to points of interest, parties and home visits. After several months of this, I dropped in on a Saturday afternoon watermelon feed. Before long the ringleader of the boys in the cottage pulled me aside and in great seriousness said, "Tell me, Chaplain, what's their angle? Why are they doing all this stuff for us?" After some discussion of his suspicions, I asked if he thought that they might be genuinely interested in him and in the other boys. He scoffed at this idea, saying, "You know everyone has an angle. But I just can't figure what their angle is."

Is the struggle against grace a problem primarily for nominal believers who suffer illness and for deprived children who fear the love of adults? May we not assume that persons who are totally committed to the religious life will be free of this perverse and contradictory distrust of both human and divine grace? I submit as evidence to the contrary the fact that many clergymen work better when motivated by competition than by compassion. Both in counseling and in clinical training ministers report private misgivings about their motivation for religious work. Often a man says, "I know that I do my best work when I am angry—when I have something to fight against. Even my deeds of compassion are colored by my competitive drive—my drive to rack up a few more statistics for the record." Ironically, many a denominational campaign for funds to support a charitable cause such as denominational hospitals or pioneer missions has been powered by the appeal to prevent some rival religious group from taking over the field.

We act as if grace were not enough in the religious life, as if gratitude were a weaker motive for ministry than competition. Character guidance and religious education display a similar distrust of the effectiveness of grace. Here the appeal to duty, to the keeping of the law, is often employed more vigorously than the communication of acceptance. Forgiveness presupposes judgment. Law must be known and respected—and violation confessed—before grace can be received. But if grace is not experienced, the religious life crushes us instead of setting us free.

How, then, shall we understand the purpose of pastoral ministry? If it is to be understood as a preparation of the way for divine-human encounter in which grace is communicated and reconciliation experienced, in what sense does the pastor prepare the way? Are his techniques of listening and acceptance more effective than his reading of Scriptures and offering of prayer? Perhaps his task is to speak about the ultimate Word with little regard to the quality of interpersonal relationship between himself and his parishioner. May we place an absolute value upon either alternative or a combination of both? Should the pastor make his message explicit or rely on its being implicit in the pastor-parishioner relationship? Is any method or combination of methods ultimately effective in preparing the way for divine-human encounter? These questions call for a comparison of the methods of pastoral care and counseling with other methods of ministry within the church and with the methods of the helping professions outside the church.

CHAPTER THREE

WHO HAS The LAST WORD?

The experiencing of God's grace is the ultimate goal of pastoral care and counseling. But what is the immediate goal of counseling? How shall the purpose of counseling be defined in operational terms? The ultimate goal of ministry is beyond our power to control or predict, but immediate goals are clearly within reach. The problem we face now is to determine whether one form or style of ministry is more effective than others in preparing the way for divine-human encounter in the midst of human crises.

Ministers are educated to interpret and proclaim the Scriptures. Congregations expect their ministers to be persuasive preachers. They expect us to know the last word and to speak the last word. Protestants generally assume that preaching is the last word in the preparation of the way for divine-human encounter. This assumption needs to come under the dual scrutiny of theology and psychology, but it cannot be examined within the scope of the present work. Focal for us is the dilemma we find ourselves in when we leave the pulpit and enter a counseling interview or make a hospital call.

We bring with us a high degree of competence as interpreters of the Scriptures and as speakers for God. We are confident that our words about the Word of God will be effective. The praise of our congregation for last Sunday's sermon still rings in our ears. We enter the world of the sick and the troubled, and our words fall upon deaf ears. We are ineffective. Divine-human encounter seldom occurs in relation to our ministry. We have not prepared the way of the Lord.

We may plunge into the study of pastoral care and counseling with its orientation toward the behavioral sciences. Surely here we will find the last word about how to prepare the way for divine-human encounter in the midst of human crises. We learn to communicate acceptance in the context of interpersonal relationships rather than merely to talk about God's acceptance of us. Honesty requires that we admit, however, that, even though we effectively communicate our acceptance of another, we cannot guarantee that the other person will experience divine grace in the context of the relationship.

We may communicate understanding to another, but we cannot be certain that the other will feel himself forgiven and affirmed by God. We may effectively interpret to a parishioner the psycho-dynamics of anxiety in his experience of temptation. Though his anxiety may diminish, we have no guarantee that temptation will be less persistent or less real. We may read the Scriptures and offer prayer in the context of a trusted relationship, and we may do so freely —not driven by unconscious needs to enhance our personal or religious authority. Still, we cannot be certain that the words will be received as a divine Word. In crisis experiences, no form of ministry has the last word—not even the last word about how to prepare the way for the experience of the ultimate Word of God.

Here is the dilemma many pastors face: Two styles of ministry contend for the favored place in shaping our pastoral ministry in crisis situations. One is the method of proclamation; the other is the method of participation. The former is built on a homiletical model and has the aura of tradition around it. The latter is built on a psychotherapeutic model with a contemporary, medical flavor. A theological perspective on this dilemma undercuts the intellectual ground for feelings of superiority of either toward the other. It smashes efforts to justify exclusive, imperialistic attitudes on both sides of the issue.

A theological vantage point from which to consider these two methods is provided by Dietrich Bonhoeffer, a German pastor, theologian and martyr under the Nazi regime. Bonhoeffer spoke to the problem under the terms ultimate and penultimate. What I have described as the content of divine-human encounter, that is, an ex-perience of grace, Bonhoeffer discusses as the ultimate or last word. The last word is justification by faith. It does not yield to the manipulation of any religious ritual or psychological process. He says that the ultimate word

excludes any method of achieving it by a way of one's own. There is no Lutheran method and no Pauline method of attaining to this final word. . . . The qualitatively final word excludes every kind of method once and for all.[1]

Penultimate refers to "things before the last thing" or the preparation of the way for justification by faith. The next to the last word may be implicit in the satisfaction of bodily hungers, in the healing of diseases or in attending church. The penultimate includes all the things that aid in providing the route over which God travels in coming to man. One cannot know in advance that the feeding of the hungry, the healing of the sick or the experience of worship will prepare the way for God. One knows the next to the last word only when the last word is spoken. The preparation of the way to divine-human encounter is known as a preparation of the way only in retrospect. To say that the penultimate is known only in the light of the ultimate is not to say that we should ignore the penultimate. Paradoxically, the method of preparing the way cannot be known positively in advance, but the effort to prepare the way cannot be neglected if we are faithful ministers.

Bonhoeffer undergirds pastoral counseling in his awareness that emotional and physical suffering impedes the reception of grace.

> There is a depth of human bondage, of human poverty, of human ignorance, which impedes the merciful coming of Christ. . . . There is a measure of entanglement in the lie, in guilt . . . in one's own works and in self-love, which makes the coming of grace particularly difficult.[2]

Bonhoeffer challenges pastoral counseling by observing that one often equates the penultimate with the ultimate. We see this in those who make easy translations between emotional health and redemption, who gloss over the reality of sin by calling it sickness and who mistake adjustment to difficulty for surrender to Providence.

The next to the last word, the word which prepares the way for divine-human encounter, may be implicitly communicated in a private relationship or explicitly proclaimed from a pulpit. It may be communicated sacramentally or scientifically. The way may be

[1] Dietrich Bonhoeffer, *Ethics* (New York: The Macmillan Company, 1955), p. 82.
[2] *Ibid.*, p. 93.

prepared through one's participation in marital conflict or marital bliss, through the work of the world or through worship, through disease and impending death or through the recovery of health and restoration of life.

No one has the last word; yet everyone may have the next to the last word. No method of ministry fences the way by which God comes to man. No human words, not even the recital of Scriptures, necessarily communicates the divine Word. Although no one form of ministry is in itself ultimate, all forms of ministry may be penultimate.

This conclusion undercuts the efforts of preachers to imperialize over counselors and of counselors to dismiss the ministry of the preacher. It challenges smugness and self-satisfaction in all its forms, including the ordained minister's feelings in relation to the layman. But, attitudes of mutual respect and genuine humility do not in themselves solve the working pastor's problems. The pastor must decide over and over again how he shall function in seeking to prepare the way for God to meet a particular parishioner in a specific situation. The pastor's decisions must be concrete and particular; they must be made in a web of related factors—none of which is ideal or clearly understood.

The contemporary, medical model for ministry assumes that the penultimate method of choice is that which is most likely to effect health. Health is understood here in empirical terms as it is defined in medicine, psychology and social work. Theoretical considerations for adopting the health goal as normative will be presented in the next chapter. At this point I shall present a case study in which faithful pursuit of the goal of emotional health was accompanied by marked changes in the person's attitudes toward God.

Chaplain Jack Bell wrote four verbatim records of his visits with Mrs. Bill Martin (referred to below as Jane) during a 10-day period. Jane's husband was a terminal cancer patient in a general hospital. He had been ill for two years, most of which time he was hospitalized. According to Jane, the family had spent more than thirty thousand dollars during her husband's illness. She had sold their home and used all their savings. Their funds were depleted. Jane, about 50 years of age, was employed as a secretary. Bill, her husband, was comatose most of the time. Prior to his illness he had been a handsome, outdoor-type man.

C.1 (Abbreviated designation for Chaplain Bell).

(I went to the door and there was a "Do Not Knock" sign, so I had one of the nurses call Jane out in the hall for me.)

Hello, Jane. I just wanted to stop by and see how things were coming along.

P.1 (Abbreviated designation for Jane, the patient's wife).

Oh, I don't think he is ever going to die. This is going to go on forever. The doctors aren't going to let him die. When one thing plays out they use another, and it is all just a senseless waste. I wouldn't mind if there was a hope that he could get well, or if the doctors could learn something, or if they could teach somebody something, but they can't, and it is all such a senseless waste. What would you do in a case like this, Jack? Do you see any sense in it? It's just like pouring money down a rat hole.

C.2 Well, Jane, I have never been in a situation like yours. So my answer wouldn't mean very much to you.

P.2 You just *can't* know how you'd feel unless you had been through it like I have. People come up here and they expect me to be vibrant and cheerful and interested in things. But I don't care about anything anymore. I don't even eat or sleep anymore. One of the doctors gave me a sleeping tablet to help me rest a while ago, but I wore out on them a year ago. They don't have any effect on me at all now. I have sent for him to give it back to him. The other day it was misting, and after work I was coming in on the freeway, driving 75, and a truck swerved over into my lane, without giving any kind of a signal, and just missed me by inches. Most people that would have scared to death. But it didn't even phase me at all. You know how that would ordinarily make your stomach knot up? (I nodded.) Well, I didn't feel a thing.

I used to be a person who was interested in everything—had lots of hobbies and things, but nothing interests me anymore. Not even my work. I used to take such a delight in it, but now I don't even care.

C.3 I'll bet that you can't even cry.

P.3 No, I don't even cry anymore. I don't even love Billy anymore. He's not the Billy I knew and loved. He's just a thing, lying in the bed, that has drained everything out of me. I don't have any emotions. It seems like I'm way up here looking down on all this, completely set apart from it, almost as if it weren't really happening to me. Can you see any sense in all this, Jack?

C.4 You're having a hard time finding any sense in this.

P.4 It's just such a senseless waste. I don't even have any feeling toward the doctors anymore. I used to just despise Dr. Thompson, but now I just don't care. They are killing three persons

instead of just one. I'm going to die before Billy ever does, and
my sister comes up here. She really doesn't have to, but she does
—until she has terrific migraine headaches when she gets home;
and she has to stay in the bed most of the time.

C.5 You have been telling me that you no longer have any feeling;
yet from the other things you have said it sounds to me like they
are hurting so badly that you won't let yourself feel them.

P.5 I guess things do hurt, but I don't feel them. [Pause]
We're going to try to take Billy to the charity hospital around
the first of next month, or maybe sooner if possible. All our
money is gone and we're going to have to do something. I've
left a note for the doctor, so we'll know more about it tomorrow.

C.6 You mentioned that you felt "way up here looking down on it
all." But you seem to have enough touch with reality to know
that you have to do something to ease the financial strain.

P.6 Yes, we've got to do something. I wish that we could have
gotten him into the cancer hospital when this thing first started,
but I guess it's too late now. They're not interested in taking on
terminal cases. There isn't any way that you could get him in
is there?

C.7 No, I don't think so. You'd probably have more influence in
that than I would.

P.7 This is all such a senseless waste. I wish that the doctors would
let Billy go ahead and die. But no. They've got to kill three
persons instead of one. It's going to kill three of us instead of
just one. Well, thank you for coming by, Jack. But there is
nothing that you can do to help. There is nothing anyone can
do to help. (She turned to go inside.)

C.8 Good-bye, Jane.

P.8 Bye.

Chaplain Bell's own evaluation of the interview follows just as he
wrote it at the time:

This lady has more emotional pain than I think I have ever seen
in a person who is still functioning in society. She has so much pain,
in fact, that she has almost withdrawn completely from her situation
on a feeling level. This is evidenced in P.3 where she indicates that
she is "way up here looking down on things." The pain that she feels
is so massive that she is forced to suppress it all out of awareness lest
she be completely overcome by it.

She says that she doesn't care about anything, and that nobody can
understand what she is going through, and that nobody can help
her, and she rebels at people who try to help her. The private-duty

nurse said that she had said to Jane, "How are you?" and that Jane
had answered, "Don't ask me how I am, ever." However, I interpret
this pushing people away and saying that she can't be helped as a
desperate cry for help and understanding on a profound level.

In this interview I tried to communicate to Jane that, although I
had never experienced what she was going through, I was aware that
she was having real pain almost to the point of losing touch with
reality. In a sense, I was trying in one way to represent the reality
of the situation to her: C.6 for example.

P.7, where she said that there was nothing I could do to help, I
interpret as saying that she was in need of help, but that no one
seemed to be able to understand or really care what she was going
through. "I need help, but I don't know what anybody could do for
me. No one has been really interested in me enough to understand
me." It was also sort of saying, "Don't come back and bother me
unless you are willing to try to understand me without giving me
pity."

I think that she needs someone to be sensitive to her feelings of
hurt and pain, and to give her enough support so that she can deal
with them gradually without being overcome by them. This is a
really big order, and I'm not sure how well or how much I will be
able to help.

In this interview Chaplain Bell was faced immediately with the
issue of what penultimate method to use in seeking to prepare the
way for divine-human encounter. Should he attempt to communicate the gospel of God's love, of grace sufficient, in an explicit or an
implicit way? He decided to rely on the interpersonal relationship—
to communicate the gospel implicitly. In Jane's opening statement,
P.1, she tested him by asking, "What would you do in a case like
this, Jack? Do you see any sense in it?" Chaplain Bell wanted to
meet her honestly, but he knew that answers—especially theological
answers—to questions like these could not deepen their relationship.
He replied, therefore, with a simple but honest statement in C.2:
"Well, Jane, I have never been in a situation like yours. So my
answer wouldn't mean very much to you."

Again in P.3 and P.6 Jane tests Chaplain Bell. First she invites
him to share his theodicy—to justify the ways of God to her. Next
she asks him to do something for her—to be a substitute social
worker. Both times, C.4 and C.7, Chaplain Bell refused to be de-
flected from his central goals: to offer her a relationship of under-

standing, to enter her feelings empathetically at as deep a level as possible.

The interview ended abruptly with a religiously ragged end as Jane turned away saying, "There is nothing that you can do to help. There is nothing anyone can do to help." Chaplain Bell does not try to tie up the ragged end with prayer or some form of religious reassurance. He accepts her despair, her practical atheism, and her personal rejection of him and says quietly, "Good-bye, Jane."

During the next few days, Chaplain Bell also visited with Jane's sister. A few statements (the first interchange of conversation has been omitted) from this interview are especially revealing:

C.3 How is Jane doing?

PS.3 (Patient's sister-in-law).
Oh, she's as hard as ever. She was kinda mad at me this morning when she left. But I'm getting used to it by now, so it doesn't bother me. But she did the most awful thing last night. Our minister came up to see us and she told him, "Don't ever talk to me about God again. I just don't want to hear all the stuff about love and mercy. Just don't talk to me." That was just awful. . . . It is awfully embarrassing and painful for him. Don't you think that Jane was just awful to him?

C.4 He probably understands what Jane is going through and didn't take it to heart.

PS.4 . . . Any help we give we have to sneak around to do because Jane won't let us give her anything.

C.5 She's trying to bear the whole burden by herself?

PS.5 Yes, and she has become so hardened.

C.6 Perhaps this is her reaction to her trouble. She has hardened herself to it in order to keep it from completely overcoming her.

PS.6 Perhaps that is so. But I can't see how she can do it. We just can't do it alone. We have to have faith. [Pause]
I would like to help her, and so many other people would, too. But she just won't let anyone help her.

C.7 Sometimes we help most by not trying to help, but just understanding.

In a second visit with Jane, Chaplain Bell reports that for the first time she expressed a positive feeling. She took the chaplain's hand and said, "Jack, it has been so nice of you to come by. You have meant so much to us." She reported the hostile encounter with her minister which her sister described (*PS.3*). Her reference to this encounter came immediately prior to her expression of gratitude for the chaplain.

Chaplain Bell's evaluation of the session included the following:

> I am amazed by the change of attitude which is evidenced in this visit as compared to the last one. I am also pleased with her response to me personally. I have been puzzling over the difference between her rather warm response to me as compared with her rather cool and rejecting response to her own pastor. I am unaware of her pastor's approach to her, so I can only evaluate my own. I have tried to do two things: (1) Be understanding and sensitive to her own feelings of hurt and pain, and the defenses which she uses to keep them from destroying her. (2) Indicate my interest in her by showing interest in her husband.

It is becoming clear that Jane is driving people away from her so that she may better encapsulate her emotional pain. She has attacked the private-duty nurse, the doctor, her pastor, her sister and other relatives. In contrast to them, the chaplain is the only person who has not attempted to offer her some kind of help in the usual sense of the word. He has offered no positive ideas, no religious reassurance. He has neither read Scripture nor offered prayer. He has faithfully given her just one thing: an experiencing of her own feelings with her. Jane's brief word of gratitude is a sign of change which is about to color her feelings in a pervasive way.

The next interview was held in the hall. Billy was in critical condition, but he had rallied. The doctor said that the only thing keeping him alive was his will to live. A brief segment of the interview follows:

> *P.6* . . . I couldn't stand it if I were you and had to get up in the morning and know I was going to have to face so many people's grief and suffering.
>
> *C.7* Well, we can't exactly share the grief and suffering. I mean, we can't grieve or suffer for people because we aren't actually going through it.
>
> *P.7* Of course, you can't. But you give your support to them and show your interest in them, and that means so much. The interest that you've shown us *and that all the people here have shown us* has meant so much.

. . . I think every hospital ought to have a chaplaincy program. It does so much good for the people who are in suffering and grief. [Pause]

Chaplain Bell's evaluation sums up the contrast in Jane during this ten-day period:

I feel that there has been a marked if not drastic improvement in Jane between the time of the first verbatim and this one. In the first interview she had attempted to detach herself from everything and everyone. She said such things as: "I don't think that he'll ever die," "They're killing three persons instead of just letting one die," "I don't have any emotions," "I feel like I'm way up here looking down on all this," "There is nothing you can do to help—there is nothing anyone can do."

By way of contrast, in this interview she indicated admiration of her husband; interest in other people; appreciation of other people's interest and concern (P.6,7); inspiration by the courageous and victorious suffering of others; acceptance of ill treatment without much expression of bitterness, and concern for her husband's welfare.

As I reflect on my ministry to her, it seems to me that the thing which "triggered off" this about-face was my willingness to listen with interest and concern to her "wrong" feelings and accept her as she was without admonishing her to change or to "buck up." . . . With regard to the progress which this lady has apparently made, all I can say is *"Praise God!"*

I wish to add only one observation. Jane's attitudes initially implied religious unbelief. They implied doubt in the Providence and goodness of God. Her minister's reference to God's love and mercy evoked from her a hostile, defiant response. It was as if she wanted to curse God but cursed the minister instead. Her attitude in the concluding conversation implies belief in God's goodness and mercy. She is grateful to a wide group of people now. She blesses instead of curses those around her. She changed direction—from hardening to softening, from increasing coldness to warmth, from tension to relaxation. Many persons in a similar situation show no reversal once the hardening process has advanced as far as it had in Jane.

This case is cited not to prove but simply to illustrate the position that the penultimate goal of enhancing emotional health is the preferred method in seeking to prepare the way for divine-human encounter in the midst of tragic circumstances.

Traditional methods deserve a hearing next. The traditional, churchly model is built on the assumption that the penultimate method of choice is that which makes the Scripture most fully explicit in the pastor-parishioner relationship. The most detailed study of pastoral care that contends for traditional methods of ministry is the recently translated work of a Swiss Reformed pastor-theologian, Eduard Thurneysen. Thurneysen advocates a homiletical approach to pastoral care and counseling. Psychotherapeutic approaches and the goal of health are vigorously repudiated as perversions of true faith and ministry. Thurneysen says, ". . . the content of pastoral care is identical with that of public preaching, but here it assumes a private form."[3] Because the pastoral conversation deals with the communication of the Word of God it is "a special discourse distinguished from profane and natural speech."[4] The "boundaries which separate pastoral conversation proper from common everyday conversation must in no way be obliterated."[5]

That which distinguishes pastoral conversation from psychiatric conversation, for example, is the deliberate repetition of the words of Scripture by the pastor for purposes of exhortation and judgment. The goal of counseling for Thurneysen is to see to it that the counselee is always conscious of his relationship to God. This is accomplished best as "the Bible is opened, the Word of God is read and interpreted, there is prayer; God is praised and thanked."[6]

Thurneysen urges pastors to listen attentively and at length to the problems of their counselees. He rejects all techniques of counseling except this one: to be a listener.

> If any instruction at all is valid in this area, it would be that one must be prepared . . . to be a listener—a patient, concentrated, attentive, alert, and understanding listener and nothing else.[7]

As we listen we are to be mentally busy evaluating the person's problems in the light of the Word of God and preparing our exhortation.

[3] Eduard Thurneysen, *op. cit.*, p. 15.
[4] *Ibid.*, p. 105.
[5] *Ibid.*, p. 113.
[6] *Ibid.*, p. 109.
[7] *Ibid.*, p. 127.

The ability to hear both the counselee and the Word of God "without a single word passing our lips" is an ability we cannot acquire. "It must be given to us. It springs from the love of Christ."[8] In his next sentence, however, Thurneysen contradicts himself, saying that this ability to hear another can be improved if we will study the Scriptures for clues to "the innermost secrets of man" and if we will "study the writings and, as far as possible, the *conversations of true pastoral counselors*."[9]

Listening, for Thurneysen, is always a means to the end of exhorting. The decisive moment in all counseling is what Thurneysen calls "the breach in the pastoral conversation."

> The conversation is conducted so as to lead to the great pastoral turning point, the disturbing and breaking of the conversation by the hearing of the Word of God.[10]

The breach is not advice giving in the sense of specific counsel about human behavior. The breach is not repressive manipulation of the counselee; it is not an effort to counsel the problem away. The breach is a removal of the problem from the human perspective to the divine perspective. It is exposure of the problem to the Word of God. "The observed facts must immediately be challenged by definite questions directed by the Word of God to everything human."[11] The breach is a shift from listening to exhorting, from acceptance to exposure, from diagnosis to prescription. The breach is the pastor's effort to stir up the counselee "to make a concrete *decision*."[12] This decision is what Sören Kierkegaard calls "the leap of faith." It is a leap into faith that one's sins are known and forgiven, that grace has done for one what his own striving could never do.

Thurneysen affirms, at some points, the study of psychology, law, ethics and sociology as aids in the development of pastoral attitudes of acceptance. But he is ambivalent about the help of the so-called "profane" sciences for the pastor's counseling ministry. His language is peppered with alarm words when he speaks of any other approach to pastoral care except his own. He speaks of Reformed theology be-

---

8 *Ibid.*, p. 128.
9 *Ibid.*, p. 129.
10 *Ibid.*, p. 138.
11 *Ibid.*, pp. 132–134.
12 *Ibid.*, p. 143.

ing "endangered" and in need of "protection." He whips exponents of alternative views by reductionism, saying their views are "nothing but" this or that. He writes like a frightened man who is seeking to build a closed system so as not to be vulnerable to the ambiguities of life. Theologically, he is the champion of the self-sufficiency of God. Clinically, he seems to be in full flight from the God who freely meets us with contradictions of our systems of belief. In pastoral care he seeks the security of dogma and ritual rather than daring to risk himself in the pastoral encounter.

Thurneysen advises pastors to be detached from their counselees. He sees the minister as a water pipe conveying the Word of God to the people. The pastor's communications to persons in trouble are analogous to the delivery of telegrams containing very important messages about the meaning of Christ's sacrificial death. He does not even consider the idea that this message may be contained in the attitudes and bearing of the pastor himself toward the troubled parishioner.

Only twice in all of his writings does Thurneysen give us clinical samples of pastoral conversation.[13] Just after the close of World War II, Thurneysen concluded a lecture on the meaning of the cross of Christ with the report of a brief conversation with a student. His report is reproduced in full, with paragraphs numbered to facilitate the subsequent commentary.

> 1. A student comes to me and speaks in stormy words of the denial of Christianity in the present world. "Where were the Christians when the war broke out? Where are the Christians today when the war continues to spread? Where is their protest, their program against social suffering? Are not the non-Christians better than the Christians?"
>
> 2. I listen to him for a long time and am silent, for I know that he is right with his complaint, that there is guilt piled upon guilt.
>
> 3. But then I interrupt him. I say to him: "Now let me put a

[13] I am indebted to Jack A. Worthington's doctoral dissertation for access to this material, since it has not been translated into English anywhere else so far as I know. I shall present the shorter of the two clinical reports with some evaluative comments. A fuller discussion is contained in the following: Jack A. Worthington, "Anxiety and Forgiveness in Pastoral Care: A Critical and Constructive Study of the Adequacy of Eduard Thurneysen's Theology of Pastoral Care and Oskar Pfister's Pastoral Analysis for Facing the Parishioner's Anxiety" (Unpublished Doctoral Dissertation, Divinity School of the University of Chicago, June, 1961).

question to you: Do you know that your sins are forgiven? What do you say to this?"

4. He stares at me. He hesitates. His flow of words halts. He asks me: "What does that have to do with my question?"

5. I say to him: "That is your business, but in any case you see that this raises an entirely different question from your questions, and I say to you: You still have not seen anything of all that Christianity means and is as long as you have not seen this question of mine. And perhaps your inability to resolve the other questions is dependent upon the fact that you and I and all the rest of us contemporary Christians are not such awful scoundrels, but that at last we have not yet really and not yet urgently enough got this question put—the question about the forgiveness of our sins—and that we can no longer dodge it!"[14]

In paragraph 1, we ask: What motivates the student's questions? He is using "stormy words." His mood suggests that he is motivated in part, at least, by the storm and stress of his inner world as well as the chaos without. Who does not feel longings for security in the chaos of the modern world? Perhaps he has been taught to expect security as a Christian's right. We do not know for sure. We only know that he is deeply disillusioned and agitated. How shall the pastor respond? If he were to respond in the manner of Chaplain Bell, he would seek to enter emotionally into the student's disillusionment and into his defiant protest against Christianity.

But Thurneysen is not really listening to the student. He is listening, instead, to his own accusing conscience. In paragraph 2, he says: "for I know that he is right . . . there is guilt piled upon guilt." Here the pastor seems to share the student's supposition that Christianity is obligated to guarantee peace and security in this world. At least he seems to feel that world wars threaten the claims of Christianity to human allegiance, that God's honor is at stake and must be defended. He rushes to God's defense. As the defender of the faith, he issues a massive defense of God against the student's charges.

To give Thurneysen the benefit of the doubt I will conjecture that his reply in paragraph 3: "Do you know that your sins are forgiven?" is meant to be, in part, a diagnosis of the student's problem and simultaneously a prescription. If so, Thurneysen sees the student's anxiety about the role of Christianity in the world to be related to

[14] *Ibid.*, pp. 175–179.

his anxiety about his personal relationship to God. This may be an accurate diagnosis. It is possible, however, that Thurneysen is diagnosing his own internal anxiety, which the student's question has triggered. Let us assume that their needs are similar enough that in either case the diagnosis is accurate. Does Thurneysen's pronouncement of the diagnosis and prescription effect a cure?

In paragraph 4, the student is stunned. He feels that Thurneysen has not heard him at all. He says, in effect: "Where have you been all the time I have been talking?" The student is cowed. He probably feels utterly rejected. Thurneysen has said that the young man's cure is in the forgiveness of God. Thurneysen has communicated not forgiveness but condemnation and rejection.

Having the advantage in the verbal battle, Thurneysen now mellows a bit and expresses solidarity in sin with the student. His confession is aborted by self-justification, however. He justifies himself by saying that we are sinners not because we failed to prevent war but because we fail to preach justification by faith earnestly enough. Thurneysen, himself, does preach justification by faith, and he does so urgently. By implication, then, he is not a scoundrel at all. He is the one who can save other Christians from their sins by calling them to preach justification by faith more urgently. Thus he covers his sins not in confession but in self-justification. If asked whether one may be justified by works, Thurneysen would thunder, "NO!" But here his work of prophetic proclamation becomes a subtle form of works righteousness. It enables him to avoid the confession of himself as sinner. The student remains among the scoundrels, however, who are focusing upon the external problems of war and peace to the neglect of the internal problems of forgiveness.

Is it possible that Thurneysen is the victim of a split between his theology and his practice of pastoral care? I think he is. The theology which Thurneysen espouses and the pastoral operations illustrated by Chaplain Bell are more coherent than may appear initially.

Thurneysen begins as the defender of the sovereignty and freedom of God. He contradicts himself by limiting the work of the Holy Spirit to the realm of a pastor's proclamation of the Word of God. This appears in several themes.

The contradiction appears first in defining pastoral care and all other pastoral functions as variant forms of proclamation. Thurneysen warns against the reification of the Holy Spirit in the hierarchical system of Roman Catholicism. He is inattentive, however, to the danger of the reification of the Holy Spirit in the traditional words of Protestantism. He even requires catechetics to be conducted on the homiletical model. He says that a pastor who is conducting catechetical instruction should be open, expecting the unexpected to occur. The methodology which he advocates, however, effectively prevents anything dynamic or unexpected from happening. He advises pastors to preach to the children or to "dictate" to them for one or two hours a week for two years.[15]

The contradiction is implicit, also, in Thurneysen's insistence upon pastoral authoritarianism. He assumes as much authority for the spiritual welfare of his parishioners as a medical doctor assumes for his patients. The pastor must both diagnose and prescribe. Analogy between medicine and pastoral care is not valid at this point. In the spiritual life the pastor participates as fully as the parishioner in the ambiguities of life. The pastor is not above sin. He is more like than unlike his troubled counselees. The authoritarianism of Thurneysen assumes that the pastor has a perspective on the life of his parishioner that is almost identical with God's perspective. Nowhere does Thurneysen make room for the pastor to acknowledge to his parishioner his own bondage to hostile and erotic feelings, to mixed motivations, to insecurity and anxiety.

Thurneysen describes pastoral care as pastoral conversation. He allows no real conversation to occur. In true conversation, a pastor risks real engagement. He risks real change in himself as a result of the conversation. He is emotionally prepared to be met by God in his conversation partner. Thurneysen speaks of this risk, but he does not, in fact, take it. He warns pastors about the danger of pastoral arrogance. But, unfortunately, he encourages arrogance by handing over too much authority to the pastor.

The contradiction inheres, also, in a radical separation of psychology and theology. Thurneysen's intention is to protect the Word from the distortions of human subjectivity. He appears to believe that the Holy Spirit will work most effectively when the pastor is unencumbered with psychological information. This makes any integrated relationship of theology and psychology impossible. More seriously, it ignores the integration which exists from creation in the

[15] *Ibid.*, pp. 29–31.

unity of man. Thurneysen affirms the unity of man, but ignores the inherent meaning of this unity. If man is a unity, his perception of God is an operation of his psychological life, which is inseparable from the rest of his operations as a person. The Holy Spirit cannot be affirmed truly or obeyed faithfully unless we recognize the subtle workings of false spirits within ourselves. Our perception of sights, sounds and odors is subject to distortion from internal emotional factors. Perception of the meaning of words and behavior of people around us is subject to distortion also. No less surely, our perception of the meaning of God's self-disclosure is subject to distortion from our mental processes—both conscious and unconscious.

Disciplined attention to human motivation and to the discerning or "testing" of the spirits (cf. 1 John 4:1) is the proper business of pastoral psychology and psychology of religion. To refuse to study personality systematically from the psychological perspective is to risk becoming hopelessly caught in one's own subjectivity without knowing it. This is to be blind with a blindness which one thinks is sight. Being unaware of one's personal, psychological dynamics and complexes may result in replacing the authority of the Word of God with the authority of the pastor. In our zeal to serve God effectively, we risk substituting the power of the pastor for the power of God's free grace.

If this critique of Thurneysen is valid, a resolution of the pastor's dilemma is in sight. We may affirm the self-sufficiency of the Word of God and the freedom of the Holy Spirit in the lives of men without being bound by the rigidity and authoritarianism of traditional models of pastoral care. We must, in fact, affirm that the theology of God's sovereignty, of incarnation in Jesus Christ and of God's continuing presence and power in the Holy Spirit are fulfilled more consistently in contemporary than in traditional methodologies so far as ministry in the midst of human crises is concerned. The irrelevance and ineffectiveness of much traditional pastoral care may inhere in this split between theology and pastoral operation.

As a resolution to one problem is found, a new question appears. If the health goal is valid for pastoral ministry as a penultimate witness to the ultimate Word of God, is it not equally valid when pursued by a medical practitioner? May not lay ministries be as valid as ordained ministries? For example, may not surgery be a preparation of the way in the same sense as a sermon? Does surgery also witness to God's grace? The witness of surgery is implicit, but so was the witness of Chaplain Bell. Is the witness of surgery resisted any more hardheartedly than the witness of proclamation in public worship? May not all lay ministries prepare the way for divine-human encounter?

CHAPTER FOUR

ARE The BOUNDARIES SECURE?

Paul Tournier, a Geneva psychiatrist, maintains that a physician must accept responsibility for two diagnoses. The first diagnosis is objective, the second subjective; the first has to do with the patient's disease, the second with the meaning which the patient finds in his experience of disease.[1] Tournier describes thereby a medical ministry that penetrates the boundaries customarily separating medical from religious ministries. Pastoral counselors penetrate the same boundary from the opposite side. As we have seen in the preceding chapter, pastoral counselors assume that in the face of human crises the pastoral method of choice is that which is most likely to effect health. The traditional methods, in contrast, seek to make the Scripture explicit.

This situation raises the question whether real boundaries exist between the psychiatrist and the pastoral counselor. If boundaries exist, are they secure? Can the boundaries be defined methodologically? Can a psychotherapist be discriminated from a pastoral counselor by examining the way he works? If boundaries exist, can they be defined theoretically? Do the differences in professionally defined purposes constitute a valid discrimination? If members of the two professions live in a no-boundary relationship to each other, how shall they live together peacefully and creatively? For most clergymen, the possibility of a no-boundary situation arouses acute anxiety about the meaning of ordination.

Men of religion often insist that life-giving and life-sustaining grace is channeled through narrow arteries to a hostile world. We now face the question: Do ordained ministers have a monopoly on the arteries? Is ordination a kind of divine corridor to all the West Berlins of human need? Do not lay ministries prepare the way for

[1] Paul Tournier, *A Doctor's Casebook in the Light of the Bible,* trans. Edwin Hudson (New York: Harper & Row, Publishers, 1960), pp. 13–14.

divine-human encounter as really and effectively as ordained ministries? Since I take the position that the last word on pastoral methodologies is a penultimate word, I conclude that the meaning of ordination does not inhere in claims of ultimate or exclusive mediation of grace.

To affirm lay ministries as effective instruments in the preparation of the way for salvation does not imply a devaluation of ordination. On the contrary, the meaning of ordination is enhanced as it is humbled. The clergyman becomes a more effective witness to Jesus Christ as he renounces for himself those prerogatives which are Christ's alone. Jesus said, "I am among you as one who serves" (Luke 22:27). He adopted the image of suffering servant. The apostles were set apart by him to the leadership of service (Matthew 20:26–28).

The apostles did not arrogate to themselves exclusive rights in the mediation of divine grace. As I understand the New Testament, they were not invested by God with such rights and authority. The apostles devoted themselves to prayer and the ministry of the word (Acts 6:4), but they affirmed the calling of all the *laos*, the people of God, to serve both the church and the world with their special gifts (1 Corinthians 12; 1 Peter 4:10–11). In terms of priorities, the modern clergyman is the servant of Christ in the church, while the laity serve Christ in the world. Theologically, the purpose of ministry is not to preserve the church but, through the church, to continue to extend Christ's service to the world. In terms, then, of honor, lay ministries outshine ordained ministries. Lay ministries are to ordained ministries what a military vanguard is to the supply corps or what the stars on the playing field are to the coaching staff.

The problem of defining the boundaries between ordained and lay forms of ministry will be dealt with here in terms of the relationship between psychiatrist and pastoral counselor at the point of meeting people in crisis. We shall view the matter from three perspectives: (1) the perspective of historically and socially defined professional roles, (2) the phenomenological perspective—actual functioning in the service of troubled people, and (3) a theoretical perspective—the essential relationship between health and salvation. The reason for focusing theoretical considerations in terms of health and salvation will become apparent as the two professions are viewed in their traditional role identities.

The Perspective of Traditional Role Identities

The differences between medical science and religion are often stated in these terms: that medicine is ultimately concerned with health whereas religion is ultimately concerned with salvation. Health means the restoration of optimal human functioning. Salvation means a divine-human encounter marked by judgment and grace and resulting in the restoration of a broken relationship between God and man. Insofar as psychiatry and pastoral counseling are identified with the purposes of their respective professional groups, the boundaries between them are clear and secure. The purpose of pastoral care and counseling, as I have defined it in these pages, links the modern pastor with his ancient predecessors. Pastoral counseling has not come to destroy but to fulfill the pastoral ministries of the past. In respect to professional purposes, the identity of the pastor is clearly distinct from the medical minister, the pastoral healer from the lay psychological healer.

The purpose of the clergyman, including the pastoral counselor, is in a general sense *sacramental;* the purpose of the psychological therapist is *scientific.* The pastoral counselor is concerned to discern reality that is beyond this world whereas the psychological therapist is engaged in discovering that which is predictable within this world. The pastor stands for a heritage in which ultimate concerns are integral to operational procedures and in which one's functioning is shaped by one's theology. The psychological investigator excludes ultimate questions from his consideration. He does this by placing brackets around man and examining only those aspects of man which are available to empirical methods of inquiry. The pastor is committed to increase among men the love of God and neighbor. The psychological therapist is committed to increase among men the understanding and experiencing of emotional and mental health. Continuity with historic traditions requires the ordained therapist to give attention to the reverence of the Creator whereas the lay therapist seeks chiefly to "subdue" the creation.

Despite loyalty to these purposes, pastoral counselors often appear estranged from their ancient heritage. The decisive issue is whether continuity or discontinuity marks the relationship of pastoral counselors to their religious community. Discontinuity obviously prevails at the level of methodology and structured thinking about pastoral ministry, but continuity prevails at the level of motivation and purpose for ministry. This continuity has been demonstrated in a number of historical studies of pastoral care in recent years.[2]

In commitment to one's professional community, the boundaries are made secure. Theology is illuminated, corrected and confirmed when theologians enter into dialogue with behavioral scientists. But theology is formed in the community of faith. In Christian terms, theology is given to the church. Pastoral or clinical theology is truly theological only to the extent that pastoral theologians and counselors are personally committed to the life of the church. Anxiety about the security of the boundaries between pastoral counseling and psychological therapy is rooted, from the church side of the issue, in anxiety about the commitment of pastoral counselors, themselves, to their religious heritage. I believe that this principle applies to psychiatry as well.

I felt for several years that ministers were more concerned about the question of maintaining the boundaries than were psychiatrists. Then I became acquainted with a psychiatric community that enjoyed only limited acceptance in the larger medical community. It was, itself, unsure of its identity with medicine. In this psychiatric community I found a high level of anxiety about the boundaries between pastoral counseling and psychotherapy. Some members of the community frankly acknowledged that their concern was irrational. Though my observation is limited, it suggests that commitment to

[2] The first historical study of contemporary pastoral counseling was Charles F. Kemp's *Physicians of the Soul: A History of Pastoral Counseling* (New York: The Macmillan Company, 1947). Three years later, Carl Scherzer's *The Church and Healing* (Philadelphia: The Westminster Press, 1950) appeared. Scherzer's history is from the perspective of Christian activity in hospital administration and nursing. The classic in the field to date is John T. McNeill's *A History of the Cure of Souls* (New York: Harper & Row, Publishers, 1951). Incisive historical essays from the perspective of the development of the Christian ministry are found in *The Ministry in Historical Perspectives*, one of three volumes in the recent series: "The Survey of Theological Education in the United States and Canada," Richard Niebuhr and Daniel Day Williams, eds. (New York: Harper & Row, Publishers, 1956). From the perspective of the development of pastoral theology since the Reformation, Seward Hiltner writes an original historical evaluation. It is in *Preface to Pastoral Theology* (Nashville, Tennessee: Abingdon Press, 1958). Hiltner's work was done prior to the Niebuhr study (1954), but was not published until 1958. These four major historical studies were completed within one decade.

the essential purposes of one's professional community and a whole-hearted sense of belonging to one's professional heritage are sufficient safeguards for the integrity of a profession. When members of diverse groups enjoy this kind of professional security, the boundaries can be crossed freely without threat and with mutual profit. Nothing is to be gained by blurring the distinction between professional groups. At the same time, nothing constructive can come from hardening these historical boundaries into a kind of Berlin Wall between helping professions. The free flow of ideas, the exchange of methodologies and the interpenetration of purposes may increase the value of each.

A Phenomenological Perspective

Discriminations between pastoral counseling and psychiatric therapy which are precise and obvious when viewed from the perspective of the history and purposes of the respective professions become blurred when clinical material is examined. To illustrate, I shall present sample interviews from both professional contexts. The professional identity of the therapists will not be disclosed until later. You might try to guess the professional identity of the therapists from internal evidence before reading the commentary.

Example A.

Anna is a 26-year-old wife of a country schoolteacher. She has been married 3 years. Prior to marriage, the couple decided to have no children during the first few years of their marriage. This was the husband's idea primarily. Four months prior to the first interview the couple decided that they were ready to have a child, but Anna is not yet pregnant.

Anna sought professional help because of strong fears that she might give birth to an abnormal child. The idea was suggested by a newspaper article, but the fear came upon her as a bolt from the blue and plagued her terrifically. She consulted a gynecologist who referred her to the therapist.

Anna is disheartened also by her husband's failure to secure a coveted new position and by disappointments with certain people in the community. She is not like her usual self.

First Interview. The therapist elicits the following information at the outset: Anna is the only child of compatible parents who treated her well. She says, "I always got along well with my mother. She died many years ago. My mother once had a nervous breakdown because of family troubles; however, she recovered without any medical assistance. She was a silent sufferer—I am, too."

Anna's husband is a capable, diligent person who works hard to get ahead. He is very active in the community and accepts all kinds of burdens. In the school, at public meetings, he is a model of behavior—calm and self-controlled. At home he permits himself to be loud and angry with his wife. She says of her relationship with him, "I am like a lightning rod." She finds this dreadful.

For a long time he did not want to hear anything about having children, "because he was afraid that he wouldn't be the only one who was loved." His jealousy is related, Anna thinks, to his having been an only child. His family life had been horrible; his parents were divorced. His mother was an ill-tempered and evil woman. He hates her to this very day. "He would like to make up, through his wife, for the love he had not received as a child."

In response to her husband and his mother, Anna feels unhappy, helpless. She has learned to be a silent sufferer like her mother. She does not show her reactions outwardly, but she admits being resentful. Her husband is annoyed by her silent weeping. Neither of them is aware, apparently, that she feels herself unjustly treated and secretly pities herself, feeling that she was used to something better at home.

After listening to Anna for some time, the therapist offers her several explanations and suggestions. In effect, he shares with her his diagnosis and gives her a prescription. He diagnoses her as one who is afraid that her own child may turn out to be like her husband and mother-in-law. She wants a child but, at the same time, is afraid of having one. Though she is not yet pregnant, something in her resists it in advance. This resistance is probably related to unconscious resentment and distrust of her husband. This unrecognized and unexpressed hostility may also account for her general depressive feelings.

By way of prescription, the therapist says that her first task is to develop a new attitude toward her husband when he flies into a rage. This requires greater honesty with herself and with him. Instead of playing the role of the silent sufferer, she must admit to herself that something in her rebels against her husband's mistreatment of her. She must admit this to herself no matter how unpleasant it may be to her pride. She, too, shares her husband's ability to become enraged; she is not above him in this. Her aggressiveness must be honestly affirmed. This is quite different from denying it and repressing it as she had done previously.

The therapist asks her to return in two weeks.

Second Interview. "Things are picking up," Anna says at the beginning of her next interview. She is full of energy and good spirits. She reports no longer being troubled by the fear about an abnormal child. It recurred only once or twice and in a very weak form after her previous visit. She also shows the beginning of a new attitude toward her husband. When he breaks into a rage, she no longer finds it necessary to weep. She says that she does not become uncontrolled but "I hold my ground." "My emotions are under control, and he likes it that way. He laughs, seems to enjoy the situation and stops his raging and shouting." He has told her, "You're pretty forceful these days." "I can speak to him in quite a different manner now and I understand his difficulties much better," Anna reports. She feels that he inherited his ways from his mother and will not get rid of them all at once, but, she adds, "I am equal to the situation."

She now affirms what was told her about self-pity: "I can throw it off, instead of indulging in it. . . . Nothing is accomplished by bearing a grudge, it only complicates things." The depressive feelings have lifted. She reports, "I have something to look forward to. Once again, I enjoy my work, have a good appetite and sleep well, although I dream a great deal."

Anna reports, also, that between the first and second interviews she regained her faith in religion. She does not say just how this happened. It emerged spontaneously. Although she had been reared in a religious home, she drifted away from her faith when she attended college. This became more pronounced since marriage, for her husband "was guided only by science, proof and reason," and she had gone along with him, offering only little resistance. She feels this was not right. Now she can receive help from Above when she herself fails. "I have faith again and can take things in my stride. However, I shall not try to influence my husband in this regard. He never received any religious training at home. In my case, my religious faith was childlike—from now on it must become more mature."

Example A is an instance of short-term counseling, consisting of only two interviews. Unconscious mental processes contributed to Anna's phobia. The methods of didactic analysis and advice which the therapist used were designed to reach Anna at the level of consciousness, however. The health goal and the religious goal are fulfilled simultaneously in Anna's experience. Anna becomes free to be emotionally honest with her husband. She can acknowledge and express her hostility. New freedom to affirm her hostile feelings means increased capacity to affirm other aspects of her essential self.

An important aspect of Anna's selfhood is her religious feeling. In the process of suppressing hostility, she suppressed religious feelings, too. Her religious feelings will offend her husband as much as overtly hostile feelings, she thinks. Anna discovers, however, that emotionally honest communication with her husband does not jeopardize their marriage. This discovery prepares the way for her to engage in emotionally honest communion with God.

Was Anna's therapist a psychiatrist or a minister?

Example B.
Beth is a 48-year-old mother of two children who has been married for 28 years to a man who has been a rather poor provider. She has been employed most of their marriage in order to stabilize the family finances. At no point in her marriage has Beth's husband given her much personal attention. Gradually she became deeply involved in her son's life. Twice during her marriage she became involved in short-lived affairs with other men. Though she confessed these affairs to her husband, he appeared not to respond except to become more passive and inattentive. A few years prior to the first interview, he became sexually impotent. Just prior to seeking help from the therapist, Beth was separated from her son. In going away to college, he made it clear to his mother that he was now emotionally independent of her. About the same time she felt herself being drawn into another affair with a man at the office in which she was employed. Alarmed by the possibility of entering another affair, Beth seeks therapy.

Initially, Beth is highly agitated, suspicious, secretive and confused. She had 15 interviews with her therapist. From this sequence, a few episodes have been selected for special note.

In an early session, Beth says that her relationship with her son "has meant more to me than any other relationship that I have ever had in my life! It's the biggest thing. Over all of my life, it's the biggest thing!"

The therapist suggested a connection between her relationship to her son and to her husband. And Beth replied, "Well maybe that is it! . . . I don't know. I hadn't thought about that. . . . I think there is something that I was afraid to—uh, uh—to put words to. . . . But I think that, uh, loving is a giving and not a taking. It seems to me that you could give of yourself. But, like sometimes with me, I would like to give to my husband, but, [pause] I'd like to love my husband—but I *can't!*"

This admission of inability to give herself to her husband is not followed by self-understanding. Instead, Beth justifies her interest in the other man by complaining that her husband does not understand how unsatisfied she is. She justifies her inability to try to be satisfied by her husband by saying that she has lost respect for him as a breadwinner and that she has never found him physically attractive.

As her defensiveness diminishes, Beth volunteers the judgment that she should not look for the same things at age 48 that she looked for at 20, but she confesses that she cannot seem to help herself. The therapist remarks, "these feelings are bewildering," and Beth returns to the theme of her inability to give herself. She says, "I have never been able to give myself all the way to anyone, really, and certainly never to my husband. I don't know anything about how men feel when they go to houses of prostitution. Somehow I always wondered if maybe they felt this way. That it was just a release or something like that—without the emotional involvement that you should have when two people give themselves to each other. This is what I wanted to feel. This is what I wanted. This is what I didn't have."

By this point, in the twelfth session, Beth has reviewed her experience of chronic frustration in marriage, the recurrence of disappointing extra-marital affairs and the emotional loss of her son as a kind of substitute companion. In the comments quoted above, Beth came close to saying that which she has been afraid to put into words all her married life: that perhaps she is incapable of giving herself wholeheartedly to another person, particularly to a man, in the intimacies of marriage and family life. By inference, she wonders if she is like a prostitute—emotionally. Also by inference, she wonders if the problem is in *her* rather than in her husband or her son or the other men.

The fourteenth session is dramatic. Beth comes in excited and pleased. She has talked with her husband. "It's the first time I've had a chance to talk with him in a long time. I was able to communicate with him a little, which is hopeful. We both agreed that we had grown apart. He didn't say, 'Well, what's the use.' He talked to me about it. We touched on things that had gone on before. I'd tell him that I think it would help a lot if he would try to understand the cause of this thing—the problem that we both are faced with. And we didn't end in a fuss or a fight or anything. So, I was encouraged."

The therapist says, "He recognized the distance, as you have done, and doesn't feel hopeless. . . ." Beth breaks in, "And not only not hopeless, but I got the idea that it really was of more concern to him than he had let me know about. I have the idea that it was something he had pushed back—but that deep down it had sort of been a concern to him, too."

Beth speaks of a new respect for her husband because of some recent business successes, and the therapist asks, "Do you suppose your recognition, appreciation, new respect for him got across to him in the conversation?"

"I think so," Beth went on. "One of the things I haven't done through this, as I told you once before . . . I've been so confused with my own problems that I didn't think too much about his problem. . . . It's not really an easy thing to think this about myself. It's just not. It's not, well, it's kind of a disgusting thing. . . . I just don't like the picture. But it seems to be that way. And what I'm wondering is why I'm able to see it. I think this has helped me a lot. And I don't know why. I can't put my finger on any one thing, other than just talking."

Soon Beth is reporting a second change which occurred in the week before this interview: "You know I was talking to you about this other person. And I have really made a definite decision that I don't want to have anything to do with this at all. And that I'm *able* not to—that it's over and done, and I don't even care. So I think that's good, too. Maybe that's the result of the other [the communication with her husband]." Beth says that she always wanted to feel free to burn her bridges behind her in relation to her affairs with other men, but she has not felt this freedom until now. "There's always been something way in the back of my mind. I guess some *hope* that maybe this would come about. And that, as far as I can see, is the only reason that I haven't left him."

Beth concludes her report of changed attitudes and relationships saying, "I *somehow think the change is in me*. Isn't that amazing!"

In the fifteenth and final interview, Beth says that she and her husband are continuing to move toward each other and that she feels more and more free from the need for other men as a means of meeting her needs. She feels that her sexual problems have been secondary to the problem of her inability to give herself to her husband, to respect him or to see how much his self-esteem had been damaged by her. She spoke of having feared that she was beyond hope of change and reflected that what had happened in her must be due to the grace of God.

Now, who were the therapists in each case? Example A was the work of a noted psychoanalyst, Alphonse Maeder,[3] and Example B was the work of Mr. Murray Thompson, a seasoned minister of the United Church of Canada.[4]

Many ministers and psychiatrists have tried to define operational

[3] Alphonse Maeder, *Ways to Psychic Health* (New York: Charles Scribner's Sons, 1953), pp. 15–23.

[4] At the time of this counseling, Mr. Thompson was a Resident in Pastoral Counseling in the Institute of Religion, Texas Medical Center, Houston, Texas.

differences between counseling and psychotherapy. Church bodies and psychiatric groups have appointed committees to make clear the boundaries between the professions. But the walls fall down when real cases push against them. Phenomenologically the boundaries are either broken down or, in some places, entirely removed.

Criteria set up for discriminating pastoral counseling from psychotherapy usually include the time factor. Counseling is supposed to be marked by short-term and psychotherapy by long-term relationships. Both of the cases cited are short-term, but Example A, consisting of only two interviews, is the work of a world-famous psychoanalyst who has dramatized the possibilities of extremely short-term therapy within his professional discipline. In contrast, Example B consisted of 15 hours of counseling. If Beth had needed 50 or 100 hours to come to herself, her pastor could have felt justified in giving her the time. A pastor cannot give large blocks of time to all who seek his help, but who is to prescribe in advance when a pastor shall and when he shall not leave the ninety and nine and go out on a long, time-consuming journey in search of the one who is lost?

Another criterion frequently cited has to do with the content of the therapeutic conversations. Counseling is supposed to deal with normal concerns at the conscious level, while psychotherapy deals with abnormal behavior involving unconscious mental processes. Religion is supposed to serve man at the point of his existential anxieties—his anxiety about guilt, death and meaninglessness. Psychotherapy is to serve man in his pathological anxiety—his neuroses and psychoses. Related to content is the method of the therapist. The religious therapist is expected to use directive, advice-giving techniques and the psychological therapist to use specialized techniques ranging from Rogerian participation to psychoanalytic free association, dream analysis, abreaction, emotional re-education and the like.

The two cases cited illustrate the inadequacy of discriminations such as these. In Example A, the therapist appeals to Anna at the level of consciousness almost entirely. Dr. Maeder advises Anna to become aware of the resentment and aggression which has previously been outside her awareness. He uses traditional methods of direct diagnosis and prescription. He looks very much like the traditional clergyman who listens attentively to his parishioner and prescribes new attitudes and modes of behavior. The advice of the analyst is clearly based on his science, whereas the advice of a kindly clergyman probably would be based on his religious lore. Though Dr. Maeder dealt exclusively with health problems, Anna reported improvement in her religious life as well.

Mr. Thompson, who served Beth, used Rogerian techniques of counseling as effectively as a psychological counselor. His technique was based on psychological science as completely as was Dr. Maeder's advice. The minister's goal was Beth's emotional health. She wanted to be freed from compulsive sexual behavior, which she felt to be a symptom of gradual disintegration of her entire personality. To serve the health goal, appeals to morality and to will power had to be set aside. First and foremost, Beth needed an intimate relationship in which she could be safe from exploitation, free to lower her defenses and to turn from self-justification. She needed to look at herself honestly.

Through pastoral counseling, she came to herself. She repented in the full Biblical meaning of the word. She saw herself as she was: a self-bound person, a person afraid to give herself wholeheartedly to others. She saw herself as one who has been emotionally isolated from her husband for 28 years though living under the same roof and sleeping in the same bed. She saw herself-before-God as one who is both judged and forgiven—judged for avoiding real love and for maneuvers of self-justification, forgiven by Divine Grace which she perceived to be operative in her experience of a new freedom to give herself in love to her husband. The minister sought Beth's health, and in doing so he prepared the way for Beth's salvation in the sense of a divine-human encounter.

Is one who employs the findings of behavioral science in religious ministry any less a minister? Was the pastoral counselor in Example B less a minister because he walked with Beth as she relived traumatic memories of extra-marital entanglements, as she discovered the incestuous implications of her involvement with her son and as she dared to admit that she might be emotionally akin to those who engage in prostitution? To ask the question is to see its absurdity. Religious ministry is fulfilled not less but more completely when a pastor actually prepares the way for divine-human encounter, for an experience of repentance. To speak about divine-human encounter, to invite a parishioner to repent, is of little significance no matter how theologically correct or Biblical one may be, so long as the experience of repentance does not occur.

Example B illustrates the impossibility of a pastor avoiding unconscious mental processes in pastoral work. The issue is not *whether* one deals with unconscious processes, but *how* one deals with them.[5] Religion which is not competent to deal with the irrational dimensions of human motivation is irrelevant to man as he essentially is—as he is-before-God.

If religion is irrelevant when it ignores man's irrationality, psychological therapies are irrelevant to man as he essentially is when they ignore man's religious striving—his longing for meaning. No matter what a client's presenting problem may be, he is also asking religious questions: What is the good life? Where does it lead? How much freedom does a man have? Are the claims of religion illusion or are they insight into transcendent reality?[6]

Discriminations between pastoral counseling and psychiatric therapy may be made with only limited validity. Precise criteria do not exist for deciding who needs pastoral and who needs psychiatric care. The degree of severity of a person's emotional disturbance is one relatively useful criterion. Very disturbed persons should be seen by a psychiatrist at once. The helping person's level of professional competence provides a standard for deciding who should attempt to care for a troubled person. Anyone who presumes to be a counselor or a therapist should understand transference phenomena, for example. He should be professionally trained to cope constructively with a client's projection of inappropriate expectations upon the counselor. Questions of legal responsibility sometimes help define areas of functioning. These criteria lack precision and do not provide us with mutually exclusive discriminations, however.

If boundaries exist at all between pastoral counseling and psychological therapy, the most that can be said for them is that they are broken walls. They are walls which both psychiatrists and pastoral counselors freely disregard in their care of troubled persons. The interpenetration of pastoral counseling and psychotherapy in practice does not require that professional identities be blurred. It

[5] R. Finley Gayle, Jr., M.D., "Conflict and Cooperation Between Psychiatry and Religion," *American Journal of Psychiatry*, XIII, July, 1956. Also issued by National Academy of Religion and Mental Health, 1956, p. 5.

[6] Orville S. Walter, "Metaphysics, Religion, and Psychotherapy," *Journal of Counseling Psychology*, V, No. 4 (1958), pp. 243–252.

does not invalidate historical and social definitions of role. It provokes, however, a reconsideration of the essential relationship between health and salvation.

The Perspective of Health and Salvation

The boundaries that are broken when psychotherapy and counseling are viewed from the perspective of actual functioning do not exist at all when the goals of health and salvation are examined theoretically. From the perspective of the essential relation of health and salvation, a no-boundary situation exists. Stated propositionally: *Health is potential in salvation, and salvation is potential in health.*

Religious communities have usually been quick to claim that health is potential in salvation. This claim is sometimes erroneously interpreted to mean that whatever is religious is right. Religious behavior is not necessarily healthful behavior. Contemporary psychological studies demonstrate that religion may be pressed into the service of emotional illness as well as of emotional health. Anton T. Boisen and Carroll A. Wise were among the first clinical theologians to study religion in both illness and health. They have made careful discriminations between sick and healthy forms of religious experience. Their work confirms the view that the experience of salvation, defined in its own terms, in terms of the theology of the church, is potentially an experience of emotional health.[7]

Wayne E. Oates explicates this proposition in his recent work, *Christ and Selfhood.*[8] From both psychological and theological perspectives, he asks what happens when a man is decisively encountered by God-in-Christ? In such an experience a person is brought face to face with his own past—his history of sin. Simultaneously, his selfhood is focused on his future—his end and aim in life, both in time and in eternity. He is focused also on his present need for identity through relationship—through belonging to God-in-Christ and to the Christian community. One is confronted with his weakness and his strength, with his neglected abilities and his previously

[7] Boisen, *op. cit.* and Carroll A. Wise, *Religion in Illness and Health* (New York: Harper & Row, Publishers, 1942).

[8] Wayne E. Oates, *Christ and Selfhood* (New York: Association Press, 1961).

unrecognized possibilities. In Christian experience, one is moved to confess his sin, to confess a new identity as a Christian and to affirm that life is being shaped by a Divine purpose or "calling."

Mental health, scientifically defined, is not primarily concerned with man-before-God. Within humanistic brackets, however, definitions of mental health may be positively correlated with Oates' analysis of Christian experience. Mental health includes the assimilation of one's past, the clarification of one's identity in the context of interpersonal relationships and, in Jung's terms, commitment to one's true "vocation" as the climax of the process which Jung calls "individuation."

Less generally accepted is the proposition that *salvation is potential in health*. The examples presented in the previous section provide illustration. In Example A, the way was prepared for Anna to be encountered by God in a positive rediscovery of her religious faith. In Example B, the way was prepared for Beth to come to herself in genuine, wholehearted repentance. At the conclusion of the counseling, she confessed that what had happened was to her an experience of the grace of God. Both therapists employed methods based upon behavioral scientific appraisals of man; both were immediately devoted to health goals for their clients. The clients, in both cases, found the way prepared for religious experience.

Deitrich Bonhoeffer's discrimination between ultimate and penultimate forms of ministry provides a theological basis for saying that salvation is potential in health. This is stated rather fully in the preceding chapter. At this point, an illustration drawn from Bonhoeffer's own pastoral care of the bereaved will help to clarify the potentiality of salvation (the ultimate) in forms of ministry designed to enhance health (the penultimate).

> Let us ask why it is that precisely in thoroughly grave situations, for instance when I am with someone who has suffered a bereavement, I often decide to adopt a "penultimate" attitude . . . remaining silent as a sign that I share in the bereaved man's helplessness in the face of such a grievous event, and not speaking the Biblical words of comfort which are, in fact, known to me and available to me. Why am I often unable to open my mouth, when I ought to give expression to the ultimate? And why, instead, do I decide on an expression of thoroughly penultimate human solidarity? Is it from mistrust of the power of the ultimate word? Is it from fear

of men? *Or is there some good positive reason for such an attitude,
namely, that my knowledge of the word, my having it at my finger
tips, in other words my being, so to speak, spiritually master of the
situation bears only the appearance of the ultimate, but is in reality
itself something entirely penultimate?* [italics mine] Does one not
in some cases, by remaining deliberately in the penultimate, perhaps
point all the more genuinely to the ultimate, which God will speak
in His own time. . . . Does not this mean that, over and over
again, *the penultimate will be what commends itself precisely for
the sake of the ultimate,* [italics mine] and that it will have to be
done not with a heavy conscience but with a clear one? [This ques-
tion] . . . embraces the whole domain of Christian social life, and
especially the whole range of Christian pastoral activity.[9]

Bonhoeffer asks rhetorically, ". . . is there some good positive reason for adopting a penultimate form of ministry?" And the answer is
"Yes." The good, positive reason for adopting a penultimate form of
ministry is that God is self-sufficient, self-initiating and self-revealing.
He alone has the last word, for he is the last word. The penultimate
"commends itself precisely for the sake of the ultimate" because the
ultimate, the Word, is in the immediate, particular situation as well
as beyond it. God is both immanent and transcendent; he fills both
time and eternity; he is Redeemer as well as Creator. He is Immanuel: God is with us. In ministry we do not bring the Word of
God to another. God comes on his own initiative. We only witness
to his coming. We prepare the way. He may come from within the
other person or from beyond him or both. A penultimate form of
ministry, a ministry in which the ultimate word is implied but not
spoken, may, therefore effectively prepare the way for the divine-
human encounter for which we long.

Salvation is known, then, to be potential in the service of health
as well as in the service of the church. Salvation is potential in
surgery as well as in sermons. Salvation is potential in psychotherapy
as well as in confession. Because man lives always in the possibility
of divine encounter, the realm of the penultimate, including man's
illness and health, is always potentially the ground of an ultimate or
a decisive encounter between man and God.

Professional imperialism is passé. It is out-of-date, but not simply
because most doctors and ministers are gentlemen. Professional

[9] Bonhoeffer, *op. cit.,* pp. 84–85.

arrogance expires when one affirms the unity of man and the interpenetration of health and salvation. Theologically, both the doctrine
of man and of salvation require ministers and doctors to function
cooperatively.

We are confronted by overwhelming evidence that the person
who comes to us for ministry—whether to clergyman or to physician—is a person who is indivisible. What Daniel Day Williams calls
the principle of "linkage" is affirmed both by theologians and behavioral scientists. Mind is linked with body, irrationality is linked
with rationality and both are linked with spirituality in complex
ways which we do not understand. The principle of linkage is not
like the coupling of railroad cars. Theology and behavioral science
are not discrete entities which hook on to one another in some external way. Rather, the physiologic, psychic, social and spiritual aspects of man are *homogenized*. The professional disciplines associated
with these various aspects of human life interpenetrate of necessity.
Except in terms of social role identity, ministers and behavioral
scientists work in a no-boundary region.

The exploration of this no-boundary region, which includes behavioral science and theology, is a major theoretical task for both
groups. The ways in which salvation enhances and blocks health are
well documented. It is virtually a truism to say that emotional health
is potential in salvation. The way in which therapy opens the door
to salvation is less clearly understood. It presents us with an exciting
intellectual task.

In various ways the past three chapters have developed the view
that salvation is potential in health. The next four chapters are
fundamentally concerned with the same issue. In considering man's
plight, we wish to understand the relationship between acknowledging our problems at the level of human needs and being convicted
of our sin before God. Insight seems somehow to interpenetrate
repentance. In considering man's end, we shall continue to search
for the shape of the linkage between human potentialities and sanctification. Doubt interpenetrates faith, despair inheres in hope, the
death of values is linked with the birth of new meanings. Sharing
seems linked with confession; defiance and rebellion with commitment. The process of change in therapy shows evidence of the involvement of the Holy Spirit and of linkage with religious commitment.

CHAPTER FIVE

CONSIDER The MINISTRY To MR. MILLS

Intrapsychic discovery may prepare the way for repentance and faith. It may also prepare the way for pride and unbelief. But when a pastor or a lay minister participates deeply in another person's experience of psychic discovery, he may expect that the way has been prepared for a meaningful religious experience. Clinical experience does not prove or disprove this assumption. It expands, refines, clarifies and corrects our traditional understanding of repentance and faith, however. It illuminates penultimate forms of pastoral ministry which seek to make ready for a decisive meeting between God and man.

The Biblical record provides us with a normative understanding of Christian experience. "Repent and believe in the gospel" (Mark 1:15). With this proclamation, Jesus began his public ministry. The simple confession, "Jesus Christ is Lord," bound believers to their Lord and to one another and created the communities in which the Christian witness was nourished and shared, renewed, clarified and demonstrated.

The categories of religious experience under which we study divine-human encounter are historically determined. The relevance of these categories for contemporary churchmen emerges in the clinical context of ministry. Serious attention to actual pastoral ministry may be expected to confirm and enrich these categories. Pastoral theology does not presume to validate or "prove" the Biblical categories. It looks to the concrete instances of ministry for clarification, correction and confirmation of these categories. In pastoral ministry their meaning is not merely applied; it is more fully apprehended.

Consistent with this methodology, I shall present a case study of pastoral ministry. I shall interpret it section by section in order to keep my interpretation as close to the clinical text as possible. In

Chapter Six, the themes of repentance and faith will be discussed in a more systematic and wide-ranging manner, but essentially in relation to clinical data.

A Case Study

Mr. Mills is a 62-year-old man recuperating from a heart attack in a general hospital. He works as a design engineer for a construction firm and is a bachelor, living alone now because his parents died a few years ago. He has no religious affiliation. The chaplain intern who visits him is a Protestant minister engaged in graduate clinical pastoral education; he recorded his visits in as nearly verbatim form as possible. This is the minister's second visit.

After telling the minister that he is going home tomorrow and has decided to accept his doctor's advice to delay returning to work, Mr. Mills launches into a lengthy discussion of a book he has just finished reading about Charles V of the Holy Roman Empire. He concludes his book review as follows (the numbering is exactly as done in the minister's record):

P.6 Well, I thought it was interesting. I always enjoy reading about the past history. History is a good subject, don't you think?

C.7 I enjoy it. And from our conversations so far, I can see that it means much to you.

P.7 Well, I think that history is *one intellectual pursuit by which we can find the answers*. And it makes good reading. You take Charles V of Spain, he was a great character. He was one of those Hapsburgs with the protruding jaw. He was the king who tried to protect the Holy Roman Empire during the reformation. [Pause] I have read about Luther in this book as well. This book I have been reading was written by a Catholic, so his views may be slanted, but I think he was right.

C.8 How is that, Mr. Mills?

P.8 He says that Luther took all this thing too seriously as a young monk and that he had mental trouble. Why, you take Luther's reply to the peasants of Germany. His language was terrible. [Mr. Mills related more about Luther during this period of the visit. During this whole phase he kept telling me historical facts that seemed to have very little real relevance. Every once in a while I seemed to detect one theme that ran through all his conversation. Mr. Mills kept referring to making this an intellectual activity.]

Back in the early days they made the Christian religion the official religion of Rome. But they made it an intellectual matter rather than something that meant anything to them.

C.9 You mean their religion became an assent to beliefs, but there was no personal commitment?

P.9 Yes, that is right. A certain rational way of doing things but not believing like they should. That is what happened during the Middle Ages when the monks could argue for days on end about the number of angels on the head of a needle. And I believe that a man should use his mind.

C.10 [All of this first part of the visit, which was about 20 minutes or more, I was trying to understand what Mr. Mills was really saying behind all of his talk of history. I will admit that I was a little defensive in wanting to show Mr. Mills that I, too, possessed a knowledge of history. Gradually I was seeing his emphasis on the intellectual.]
I would imagine that you like to think things out rationally, by what you have said.

P.10 I do. I have always liked to study history, and the history of philosophy as well. I also have read in theology lots—from an intellectual position, you see.

C.11 Mainly, you took an intellectual approach to religion more than making it something you could follow?

Here is a pastoral conversation in which little religious concern is evident for the first 20 minutes. A minister might justifiably conclude that Mr. Mills was open only to social chitchat. Another minister might have rushed to defend Martin Luther from the interpretation reported by Mr. Mills. Still another minister, eager to get down to business with a man whom he knows is not a professing Christian, might have abruptly changed the subject to inquire about this man's relationship to God. In C.9 and C.10, the chaplain-intern is struggling to hear and clarify what Mr. Mills is saying about his personal religious life, about his relationship to God. The C.11 comment rings true, and in P.11 Mr. Mills confesses his bondage and his sense of sin. In the same statement he seeks to justify himself with a well-worn excuse.

P.11 Well, *I have never had much religious feeling*. It just never has affected me too much. Yes, I have read about theology and theologians all my life, but I guess I haven't followed it too well. I just never could take all the literalism that was taught me.

The minister is well on the way now. He is participating in Mr. Mills' self-initiated journey of intrapsychic discovery. Theologically, I affirm that the Holy Spirit is operative in communicating prevenient grace to Mr. Mills and simultaneously convicting him of sin. His sin appears to be a broken relation to God, related to the bondage of not allowing himself to have much religious feeling. The minister runs interference for the Holy Spirit—he prepares the way—as he continues to participate in Mr. Mills' own frame of reference.

> C.12 What do you mean, Mr. Mills?
> P.12 I guess I mean that I heard people talk about how they took everything literally and never questioned or doubted. So I tried to examine my faith. That is what a man ought to do, don't you think?
> C.13 You mean to examine his faith intellectually?
> P.13 Yes. That is what I have always done. But *I have not had much deep religious feeling*. I just could not accept that literalism that was taught.

In *P.12* Mr. Mills is on the verge of sharing his early history of religious doubt. He is a bit defensive, however, and he asks the minister for an ethical judgment upon him: "that is what a man *ought* to do, don't you think?" Perhaps Mr. Mills is not sure that he *ought* to have "examined" his faith. At least he doubts that a minister will approve. The chaplain-intern is focused exclusively on understanding the man's anxious question about what he *ought* to have done. In reality he answers the question by his response in *C.13*. The answer is, in effect, you may feel free with me to relive your experience as it was and as it is. You do not need to be anxious about how I will judge you. Judgment is not mine to administer.

In *P.13* Mr. Mills confesses the judgment he feels to be implicit in his life experience: "I have not had much deep religious feeling." He quickly adds his justification: "I just could not accept that literalism that was taught." Here is another facet of Mr. Mills' plight. Every confession of sin as a self-before-God is canceled by a self-justification as a man among men, or more particularly, as a child with his parents.

The minister encourages him to talk about childhood experiences in which he was taught "literalism" in religion. In *P.14,* omitted

here, is a lengthy review of Mr. Mills' early reading, religious doubts
and intellectual pursuits. Patiently hearing Mr. Mills' defense, the
minister continues to prepare the way for repentance and faith.
Discovery in the psychic world always requires tedious wandering
through a wilderness of defensive maneuvers or security operations,
to use Sullivan's term. The interview continues:

C.15 Mr. Mills, I hear you to be saying that you see yourself as
searching for the meaning and purpose of life?

P.15 *I am. I have always been looking.* And I have tried to find
my answers by reading and examining all the books on the
subjects. But I have not lived the life that they write about.

C.16 Yes, that is hard to do, isn't it? We can read and comprehend
all that others have to say, but it seems that it doesn't do any
good unless we can personally become involved and commit
ourselves, does it?

P.16 Well, I think not. But a man has to use his reasoning powers.
If he doesn't, he will become a mental case—I mean a mental—well, what I mean is that he won't make good use of his
mental powers. But I think that we do think about God.

C.17 Yes, I think that each man in the depth of his own being and
soul does long for God and wishes to follow him. And I hear
you to be saying that you are searching for God, for the
meaning and riddle of life.

P.17 That's right. That's right. *Yeah, I guess I still am searching for
the meaning of life.*

C.18 Maybe you could tell me what your experiences have meant
to you so far in life, Mr. Mills?

P.18 Well, I have always used my reasoning powers—ever since I
was a small boy, you see. I thought that the way to getting
around having an emotional approach to religion was to have
it systematically worked out. That is why I like to study
theology. They have it all worked out in a system, and I like
that. But I didn't want any of that emotional stuff that they
tried to teach me.

C.19 You mean your parents?

P.19 Yes, my parents. They were always emotional about religion,
but they were too emotional. I guess I just didn't want to be
like them. So, I tried to read all I could and systematically
plan it out.

C.20 I get the feeling, Mr. Mills, that all this didn't or hasn't completely satisfied you. Is this what you are saying?

P.20 Well, I never have had much deep religious feeling. Maybe
some people don't have as much as others. *But I wasn't satisfied completely by all my reading.*

Mr. Mills confesses himself to be a seeker after God (*P.15, 16, 17* and *20*). He acknowledges again his bondage. His bondage consists of a lack of religious feeling and a lack of integration between his religious ideals and his actual behavior. What is new is that this time he drops his self-justifying appeal to faulty parental training (*P.15, 20*). Instead, he confesses that he has studied theology as a substitute for religious commitment, *P.18.* He becomes more aware that his theological reading has been significantly motivated by his need not to be like his parents (*P.19*). Now that his parents are dead and he, himself, is undergoing a kind of death in relation to heart disease, he sees that his theological study has not been entirely satisfying (*P.20*). Mr. Mills is confessing himself spiritually "lost" and longing to be "saved."

The religious longings of Mr. Mills appear linked to a number of psychological and sociological factors inherent in his phenomenal world. The values by which he has lived are being disorganized. In his first conversation with the minister, he expressed a growing sense of insecurity in his work. At age 62 he finds competition from young engineers quite threatening. The meaning that his work once held for him is evaporating. His company does not place a premium on creativity, and he is bored with the treadmill on which he moves at work. He has always been a "loner" but has not felt loneliness to be an acute problem until his parents died.

His heart attack undermined his confidence further by dramatizing his dependence upon others. Death anxiety is usually high in connection with heart disease. All of these stresses are fairly normal to middle adulthood, but they have become concentrated at the point of his moving into the sixties. Mr. Mills has worked hard to fulfill one developmental task of the middle adult years, namely, the formation of an adequate philosophy of life. He has read extensively in philosophy, theology and history. It is at this point that he is now most severely shaken. His philosophy of life is breaking down under the stresses of the pre-geriatric years.

It is as if Mr. Mills had built his house on the sand, in the language of the Biblical simile, "and the rain fell, and the floods came, and the winds blew and beat against that house, and it fell; and great was the fall of it" (Matthew 7:26–27). His slip of the tongue in *P.16* suggests that the disorganization of values occurring in Mr. Mills is being experienced by him as a kind of breakdown of his whole personality. He says, "But a man has to use his reasoning powers. If he doesn't, he will become a mental case. . . ." (P.16). He corrects himself, but goes on to say that his religious doubt helped him differentiate himself from his parents (P.19). Now that his parents are dead, religious doubt no longer serves this positive value in the psychic economy of his life. In its place he would like to build some religious assurance. Thus, he says, in P.20, "But I wasn't satisfied completely by all my reading."

To this the minister replies:

> C.21 You mean, perhaps, that all your intellectual pursuit for the purpose of life has been meaningful, but perhaps you still need to make some emotional response to God?

One may wonder if the minister is truly participating with Mr. Mills now or if he is introducing from his own frame of reference an evangelistic appeal "to make some emotional response to God?"

The theme of commitment appeared first in C.9 in conversation about Christianity under Constantine. But here the theme is clearly a reflection of Mr. Mills' own statement that Christianity was "an intellectual matter *rather than something that meant anything to them.*" The chaplain-intern has been proved right in assuming that Mr. Mills' references to historical Christianity are veiled descriptions of his personal experience. Thus in C.11 and C.16 the minister translates Mr. Mills' longing as a longing for commitment. In each instance this interpretation is affirmed by Mr. Mills.

A more serious challenge may be offered to the minister. We may ask why he did not take this opportunity to proclaim the good news that our longings for meaning in life are fulfilled in Jesus Christ? Mr. Mills is turning away from his futile, intellectualistic efforts to find God. Why does the minister not speak of Jesus Christ? Why does he not attempt to persuade Mr. Mills to turn to him in faith? The way would then be prepared for repentance which involves both a turning away from and a turning toward. This could be the decisive moment for confession of faith and for commitment to God in Christ.

The minister could remind us that this interview occurred in the midst of Bible-belt culture. The content of Christian proclamation is as well known to the patient as to the chaplain. Furthermore, Mr.

Mills has repeatedly said that his parents were overly expressive about their faith and that his lack of commitment was linked with his need not to be like them. The minister intuitively respects the laws of psychic life that are operative in Mr. Mills on the basis of his personal history and his cultural milieu. The minister also knows that all men are bound by psychic structures of resistance to change. This is what some psychologists call self-consistency. Mr. Mills immediately draws back from the prospect of religious experience to maintain self-consistency.

P.21   Yeah, yeah. I guess all this hasn't gotten me all that I wanted. I am getting along in years, though, so I imagine that is the way I will always be.

C.22   How is that?

P.22   Well, I am so used to making an intellectual approach to all this that I don't know if I could ever change. I'm getting old and set in my ways now and I don't know if I could change.

C.23   I get the feeling, Mr. Mills, that you might like to change from this intellectual pursuit to one of committing yourself emotionally to a higher power.

P.23   Well, I think that I have thought about it some. But like I said, I just never had much religious feeling. I don't know or haven't known which part of a man comes to know God. I don't know if it is his mind or soul.

C.24   What do you think?

P.24   I don't know. I have been told it was a man's soul and not his mind, but I just don't know.

C.25   Mr. Mills, it seems that there are persons who are only interested in a man's soul instead of his whole self. But we should be interested in everything about the person. Take for instance you, while you are here at the hospital. I could come in and only be interested in your soul, but I think it is more than that. I have tried to be interested in you as a person. And that includes your illness, or physical, as well as your intellectual and spiritual self.

P.25   Yeah, that is how it ought to be. But my parents were only interested in the soul and the emotional response. I thought they were wrong so I guess I went to the other extreme. And since I never have had much religious feeling, I don't know if I ever could have any.

C.26   Mr. Mills, I understand you to be saying that there is still a longing within yourself for this religious feeling. Yet, you are wondering if it is too late to really experience it. Is this what you are saying?

P.26 Yes, I guess it is. You see I never have gone to church much,
and all this is something that you have to get in the habit of
doing. Once we start habits they are hard to break, but if we
haven't started them, they are hard to start. But maybe I could
go to church once in awhile.

It is noteworthy that at C.23 the minister failed to participate in
Mr. Mills' ambivalence. The fear that he might not be able to
change is ignored by the minister. Immediately thereafter, by introducing an intellectual quibble about the mind and the soul (P.23),
Mr. Mills resists the chaplain's suggestion that he commit himself
emotionally to a higher power. The minister responds by focusing
on the quality of the immediate relationship. Then, at C.26 he
expresses the full force of Mr. Mills' ambivalence. At this point
Mr. Mills is able to explore the positive side of his ambivalent feeling. He considers a concrete move toward religious experience, saying, "maybe I could go to church once in awhile" (P.26).

C.27 Yes, it is hard to start habits like going to church. But I think
that there is deep within each of our beings the desire and
ability to respond to God regardless of how young or old.
P.27 Well, that is probably right. Maybe there is something within
each of us to let us respond to God. I have always tried to do
so by some intellectual system, but they never give the final
answers. [Pause] Well, we have really been talking about
some deep things today.

At this point the minister seeks to reinforce Mr. Mills' desire for
change. He affirms his faith that within everyone is "the desire and
ability to respond to God regardless of how young or old." Here is
an explicit witness to the minister's faith. For the first time the
minister shifts his focus from Mr. Mills' feelings to his own thoughts.
Notice the minister's choice of words: "I think. . . ."
An implicit witness might have been expressed by a comment such
as this: "You are wondering how you might start to change?" In
my opinion, the implicit witness would have facilitated continued
exploration of Mr. Mills' new self concept—a self open to religious
feeling. As it was, Mr. Mills agreed with the minister but moved
to terminate the visit by saying (P.27), "Well, we have really been
talking about some deep things today."
The solid gains from the conversation are not lost, however.

C.28 Yes, we have. I wonder what all this has meant to you personally?

P.28 Well, I guess that most of it has been another intellectual discussion. But it has given me something to think about as well.

C.29 Oh, how is that?

P.29 Well, it has made me *wonder* if I don't have some religious feeling. I don't know still yet if I do, but it has made me *wonder*.

Mr. Mills is aware that something out of the ordinary has happened. He has not just engaged in another intellectual discussion. He has been given "something to think about" (P.28). He, in fact, has been given a new feeling—the feeling of *wonder* (P.29). He is beginning to wonder about his own unrealized possibilities for religious feeling. The word *wonder* may well carry a double meaning in this instance. For the possibility of his becoming emotionally committed to God is a source of wonder, too. He may be sensing that God is engaging him in direct religious experience now. From the moment that trust emerged between the pastor and Mr. Mills, the presence of God was sensed by them both.

C.30 [The dinner tray was brought in at this time.] Mr. Mills, I am glad that we could share together today. I want you to know that I have been thinking of you and will continue to do so. If you get a chance, let me know how you are doing sometime.

P.30 Thank you. I will.

C.31 Well, I must be going now. I will be remembering you in my prayers. Good-bye now.

P.31 Good-bye.

The interview ends in collision with one of the inevitable interruptions which hospital routines spawn. But the pastor's final word, "I will be remembering you in my prayers," requires comment.

The minister's reference to prayer may seem to be consistent with his choice of implicit in preference to explicit forms of Christian witness. In the light of the total relationship between him and Mr. Mills, this reference to prayer is inappropriate. Such a reference to prayer is commensurate with a superficial interpersonal relationship. The minister and Mr. Mills have created far more than a superficial relationship, however. As Mr. Mills says in P.27, they have moved to deep levels together. In *P.29*, Mr. Mills wonders if he does not have some religious feeling. In this comment it seems to me that he invites the minister to articulate his incipient sense of religious feeling.

No response could better assist him in the clarification of his new feelings than a formal pastoral prayer. In prayer the minister could articulate the context of their relationship as before God, lift up the patient's sense of lostness and of longing for God and lift up to God his ambivalence both in despair and in hope of change.

Prayer of this kind makes the content of the gospel explicit. Are we not subject to the charge of inconsistency? Have we not covertly introduced elements of proclamation into a pastoral relationship ostensibly built on a penultimate form of ministry through participation? Yes, the charge may be true if the minister introduces the prayer primarily out of his own needs to perform an explicit religious ministry. If the prayer emerges genuinely out of the patient's own internal frame of reference and out of the quality of the pastor-patient relationship, the charge is false. As I evaluate this pastoral conversation, a prayer such as I have suggested would not contradict the minister's purpose to participate consistently in the patient's psychic life. However, a superficial reference to prayer *does miss* the mark of pastoral participation.

This is not to say that prayer in pastoral care and counseling is nothing but a method of pastoral participation in a person's inner world. Prayer transcends the category of participation, although it does not contradict it. Prayer also transcends the category of proclamation without contradicting it.

A Celebrative Relationship

Discussion of prayer leads us inadvertently to a reconciliation of the contradiction between participation and proclamation. The contradiction was discussed at length in Chapter Four and has reappeared during the analysis of this example. Reconciliation occurs in what may be called a celebrative quality of relationship between pastor and people. Pastoral psychologists sometimes classify patterns of relationship between pastor and parishioner as hostile, extractive, withdrawing, dependent, social-superficial, apathetic and creative. On occasion a relationship may move from any of the above patterns into a mutual experience of being in the presence and purpose of God. Such a relationship emerged from Mr. Mills' social-superficial discussion of history. It is appropriate to praise God in such a moment, to celebrate his disclosure, to confess one's faith in his intention toward us and his transforming work in us. This is a celebrative relationship, and it can be reflected most adequately with the help of religious rituals of celebration.

The psychic reality of such a moment is communion. In Communion the gospel is both demonstrated and declared; the good news is communicated both through participation in a community of faith and through proclamation of the ancient story of incarnation, atonement and redemption. The elements and their symbolic meaning cannot be fully and finally discriminated in such a moment. The penultimate mode of pastoral ministry through relationship and the ultimate word become one. The activity of the Holy Spirit is evident.

The minister's final comment in evaluating his work with Mr. Mills is this: "I have no further plans, as Mr. Mills is going home, but *I hope the ministry of genuine interest and concern will have had some lasting effect.*"

If this is, as I believe, a celebrative kind of relationship, the minister's hope is well based. I would modify his statement, however, to say that *I hope the ministry will continue to have lasting effect.* For I believe that ultimately the effect is not in the "genuine interest and concern" considered phenomenologically but is in the evident presence and activity of the Holy Spirit for whom the way was prepared by the minister's "genuine interest and concern." The continuing effect for which we hope depends ultimately not upon us but upon the initiative and authority of God.

CHAPTER SIX

PREPARE The WAY For

REPENTANCE And FAITH

Sören Kierkegaard wrote, "that if real success is to attend the effort to bring a man to a definite position, one must first of all take pains to find *him* where he is and begin there."[1] Pastoral counseling is built on this insight. If the purpose of pastoral counseling is to prepare the way for salvation, the pastoral counselor should know the plight from which his parishioner needs to be saved. He should understand the possibilities toward which salvation drives. His pastoral ministries need to be informed by serious attention to both man's plight and his possibilities. I shall attempt in this chapter to discuss repentance and faith in terms of man's plight and his possibilities as a self-before-God.

Man's Plight

Man's plight is that although created in the image of God, for relationship with God, *the relationship is broken*. This brokenness is compounded by neurotic patterns of intrapsychic and interpersonal existence. Man is caught in a web of conditioned responses, complexes, cultural and cosmic determinants. His bondage complicates and deepens his plight in relation to God because it blocks his reception of divine grace. Thus despair deepens, doubt and unbelief increase and the struggle against grace becomes, in turn, more desperate.

We need to understand the linkage between man's plight as seen from the perspective of his relationship to God and his plight as seen from a phenomenological perspective. In relation to God, man's

[1] Robert Bretall, ed., *A Kierkegaard Anthology* (Princeton: Princeton University Press, 1951), p. 333.

plight is *brokenness*—meaning a broken relationship. In relation to his fellows and his own intrapsychic life, his plight is *bondage*—the bondage of biochemical and interpersonal determinants of behavior. Brokenness and bondage interpenetrate. Brokenness in relation to God feeds the anxieties that make for psychic bondage, and psychic bondage distorts, if it does not destroy, the possibility of relationship with God. The patterns of interrelationship are undoubtedly more complex than I am able to describe. But just as health and salvation are each potential in the other so brokenness and bondage appear to be interwoven strands in the web which enmeshes man.

Mr. Mills, who was presented in Chapter Five, suffers from brokenness in relation to God. The break is compounded in part by his psychological complex about emotionalism in religion. During most of his life he rigidly excluded religious feelings from his experience. He exaggerated rationality at the expense of intuition, thought at the expense of feeling. Lopsided psychic development solved one problem only to create a greater one. His defense against emotionality appeared necessary early in his life as a means of achieving personal autonomy. He needed to be unlike his parents in order to enhance his self-esteem as an adult. From the fact that he is a bachelor we may conjecture that he needed also to be dependent on his parents in some respects. He accomplished the difficult psychic feat of remaining dependent upon his parents without serious loss of self-esteem as an adult. In this maneuver he repressed his religious feelings (and probably many other facets of emotionality) and built his life on a partial foundation—a foundation that gave away under the impact of the normal pre-geriatric stresses of life.

Mr. Mills' plight is thus created by a combination of divine-human brokenness and of psychic bondage. Paradoxically, the possibility of psychic health and religious salvation emerge in the midst of his plight. In the experience of despair over the inadequacy of his intellectual search for meaning, Mr. Mills becomes open to the possibility of religious feeling. In openness to his long-repressed feelings, the way is prepared for repentance and faith, that is, for salvation.

Theological insights do not fully explicate Mr. Mills' plight. To see the brokenness in his relationship with God is to see an important but fragmentary part of the whole man. Medical, psychological and sociological lenses help to fill out the picture. The more partial our picture of Mr. Mills, or any other person, the less likely we are to offer him a relevant ministry. If Kierkegaard's formula is correct, the possibility of preparing the way for a truly religious encounter is remote to the extent that we are unable to find a person where he is.

The psychological lens helps us to see that one factor in Mr. Mills' plight is irrationality. We see that his relationship to God is shaped in part by the structure of unconscious as well as conscious mental processes. Mr. Mills shares with all humankind certain mental functions that are described in personality theory with a measure of accuracy and predictability. A brief summary of these structures and functions in relation to Mr. Mills should help concretize this discussion.

The concept of unconscious mental processes entered the awareness of thoughtful men at least two centuries before Sigmund Freud, but Freud described clinically the shape and extent of unconscious mental processes. In Freud's work it becomes clear that all behavior is purposive, once behavior is seen in relation to unconscious as well as to conscious mental activity. Slips of the tongue, forgetting and dreams are some of the everyday occurrences which make sense when unconscious mental functions are postulated. Psychoanalysts differ widely among themselves as to the precise workings of unconscious mental processes. Some stress biochemical components; others, interpersonal and cultural components of personality dynamics and development. Existential analysts are focusing attention today on the noetic or spiritual aspects of personality— the factor of responsible choice. Areas of consensus are not large, but they are significant. The reality of unconscious mental processes is one of the areas of consensus. Human behavior cannot be understood if unconscious determinants are ignored or minimized.

The minister who talked with Mr. Mills paid attention to the unconscious factors in the patient's communication. For 20 minutes Mr. Mills talked about history in what appeared to be a random choice of topics. The minister was totally convinced that a complex of unconscious motivations governed Mr. Mills' selection of this topic and his manner of developing it. The pastoral conversation would have developed quite differently if the minister had not known that, beyond the awareness of both Mr. Mills and himself, some repressed feelings were seeking to be communicated. As we saw in the case study, Mr. Mills' unconscious longing for the restoration of relationship with God gradually came into view as his relationship with the minister developed. Because the minister was alert to ways in which unconscious feelings appear, he was able to assist Mr. Mills in confessing his sense of meaninglessness apart from religious commitment.

The term repression was used by Freud to denote a process by which psychic experience is excluded from conscious awareness but continues to be operative unconsciously. The reality of Mr. Mills' unconscious life is seen in a slip of the tongue in which he referred to himself as a "mental case." This gives us a hint as to the size and force of his unconscious anxiety.

Harry Stack Sullivan, one of Freud's revisionists, pointed to anxiety, derived from the threatened loss of satisfactions and security, as the dynamic source of behavior. Repression, which he called selective inattention, accompanies experiences of anxiety in which one senses a major threat to his self-esteem. Anxiety is a feeling of dread or horror. It is an uncanny feeling causing acute psychic pain. It is absolutely intolerable and thus requires immediate relief. Feelings of hate and of lust are more tolerable than is anxiety. Impulsive, self-destructive behavior is more welcome than anxiety. Anxiety affects a person's metabolism. This is readily evident in blushing, dry mouth, sweaty palms and the like. Anxiety also motivates the security operations, or what Freud called defense mechanisms.

Mr. Mills' justification for having resisted religious feelings through his life is that his parents were overly emotional about religion. It became obvious to Mr. Mills, himself, as the conversation progressed that this was a rationalization. The minister knows that rationalization is one of the common mechanisms of defense against anxiety. His task in ministry is not, therefore, to argue with Mr. Mills, saying that he is not justified in blaming his parents. His task is to offer Mr. Mills the kind of acceptance that will enable him to lower his defenses, risk a greater degree of threat to his self-esteem and simultaneously risk discovering that a man's self-esteem need not be based entirely on his own merit. In relation to the minister, Mr. Mills discovered that he could be valued unconditionally. He was not even being valued as a "soul" to be saved, but as a person who in his totality had withdrawn from an emotional commitment of himself to God. As far as the minister is concerned, Mr. Mills can continue to flee divine-human encounter without risk of rejection by the clergyman. The pastor's acceptance is not equivalent to Divine Grace, but it is analogous. It prepares the way for Divine Grace.

Viewed theologically, Mr. Mills' defense mechanisms have been pressed into the service of *willing defiantly to be a self-before-God.* Many persons exercise a will not to be a self-before-God. They become selectively inattentive to religion. Self-esteem is enhanced through avoidance of the normative values in which religion abounds. Mr. Mills, in contrast, is an avid reader of theology, but not a committed believer. What is the shape of his self system? In what way will a religious commitment threaten his self-esteem?

Speculating a bit, I suggest that Mr. Mills' prior self concept contained strong elements of omnipotence feeling. This is consistent with his striving for absolute theological answers. Theological systems may delight him because he finds in them a faint echo of his longing to subdue God, to find in the human intellect final answers to the riddle of life's meaning. The study of theology may be less threatening to his omnipotence striving than the experience of religious commitment. Commitment involves repentance and faith; it is related to humility more than to pride; it is the fruit of surrender before God rather than of the struggle to subdue God by explaining him.

It is in this sense that I find Kierkegaard's categories useful in describing Mr. Mills as one who is *willing defiantly to be a self-before-God.* He defiantly clings to the psychic pain of recalling his parents' excesses of religious emotionalism and literalism. He shakes this painful memory in the face of God, as it were, in order to justify himself for living in a broken relationship with God. The anxiety of risking the loss of whatever self-esteem he has built and protected through the years is more painful than the old memories of parental excesses. The anxiety of change is, in this instance, the threat of religious rebirth. A minister who is not sensitive to the shape and intensity of Mr. Mills' psychic pain is not likely to be effective in helping him to move through it. Argument or debate would be the surest means of causing him to repress again his genuine religious longings.

Man's brokenness and bondage take many forms in human experience—sometimes of a quite different pattern than appears in Mr. Mills. Broken relationship with God may be compounded either by rebellion or resignation, pride or self-derogatory attitudes, defiance or compliance. Combinations of these contrasting patterns, in alternation or in ambivalence, form patterns of bondage which aggravate man's brokenness in relation to God.

The value of clinical observations in correcting and completing theological analyses of man's plight is illustrated in an essay by Valerie S. Goldstein on "The Human Situation: A Feminine Viewpoint."[2] Mrs. Goldstein says that masculine experience colors the theological analyses of such men as Reinhold Niebuhr and Anders Nygren to such an extent that their work is seriously limited in its relevance. To say that man's chief temptation arises from the anxiety of loneliness, alienation and finitude is to overlook those for whom the chief sources of temptation are a too easy acceptance of finitude, passivity and noncreativity. The chief sin of many is not prideful effort to make the finite infinite but the passivity which evades responsibility in "triviality, distractability and diffuseness." The exaltation of the ego as an idol becomes the bondage of some, but this description is colored by masculine experience. Feminine experience finds temptation in the "lack of an organizing center or focus, dependence on others for one's own self-definition . . . in short, underdevelopment or negation of the self."[3] Mrs. Goldstein concludes by observing that social analysts such as Riesman, Arendt and others say that society is moving toward a more feminine orientation in terms of openness, socialization, cooperativeness and reasonableness. If this is true, she cautions, "a theology based solely on masculine experience may well be irrelevant."[4]

The categories masculine and feminine are subject to misunderstanding, inasmuch as the experiences described do not correspond to the respective sexual identities. Masculinity is associated with aggressiveness and femininity with passivity. In these terms, I share Mrs. Goldstein's impression that theological literature is more articulate about the ways in which aggressive forms of neurotic bondage contribute to and perpetuate man's brokenness in relation to God than the ways in which passive forms of neurotic bondage compound man's brokenness.

The wilderness temptations of Jesus inhere in the appeal of ag-

[2] Valerie S. Goldstein, "The Human Situation: A Feminine Viewpoint," in *The Nature of Man: In Theological and Psychological Perspective*, ed., Simon Doniger (New York: Harper & Row, Publishers, 1962), pp. 151–170.
[3] *Ibid.*, p. 165.
[4] *Ibid.*, p. 170.

gressive behavior to allay anxiety. They offer what Dr. Karen Horney has called the expansive solution in contrast to the self-effacing solution to anxiety. Jesus was tempted to indulge in self-glorification and arrogant vindictiveness. In reply to each temptation, Jesus is seen affirming *the primacy of his relationship with God.*

> Man shall not live by bread alone, but by every word that proceeds
> from the mouth of God.
> You shall not tempt the Lord your God.
> You shall worship the Lord your God, and him only shall you
> serve (Matthew 4:4, 7, 10).

I believe that Jesus was without sin inasmuch as his individual patterns of psychic defense against anxiety did not become an excuse for brokenness in relation to God. He practiced the message which he preached and thereby enjoyed continuing and deepening relationship with God despite the particular form of his own psychic bondage.

The early Christian community recalled their Lord's warning also against the self-effacing solution to anxiety. The parable of the talents focuses the plight of the "one talent" person (Matthew 25:14–30). Afraid of divine encounter, this person hides what is given him in the ground. The tragedy of the parable is not so much that the "one talent" man fails to return his talent "with interest," but that his relationship to the master is broken. Brokenness occurs not on the master's return from his travels, however. It occurs while the master is away. The brokenness of his relationship is revealed, not caused, at the moment of the accounting. Evidence supporting this interpretation is in the "one talent" man's distorted perception of the master:

> Master, I knew you to be a hard man, reaping where you did not
> sow, and gathering where you did not winnow; so I was afraid,
> and I went and hid your talent in the ground. Here you have what
> is yours (Matthew 25:25).

Passivity, which is this man's psychic bondage, grows like a malignancy until it becomes irresponsibility. His bondage begets brokenness. To justify himself the man distorts his memory of the master. He becomes selectively inattentive to the capacity of the master to forgive one who risks his talents and loses them entirely. Rather than risk depending upon the grace of the master, he retreats into the safety of an obscure or hidden life and justifies himself in fantasies of the master's cruelty.

The plight of the "one talent" man is the plight of many of us in so-called religious vocations. We seek to allay the anxieties stirred by a competitive world by making ourselves lovable with qualities of unselfishness, goodness, humility and generosity. The appeal to love gives us the immunity of the benign. We rest secure in ministerial privileges and move serenely in a world of painted smiles. Like the "one talent" man, we yield little or no return on the investment of life in us. Ultimate tragedy may await those of us in whom the psychic bondage of passivity becomes justification for struggling against Divine Grace.

If man's plight consists of a broken relationship with God, which is compounded by physiologic, psychic and social structures of bondage, what are the possibilities of deliverance for man? What are the possibilities for man to be freed from bondage and restored to relationship with God? Need man be freed from bondage in order to be restored to relationship with God? Need man be restored to relationship with God in order to be freed from bondage? What linkage exists between man's freedom from bondage and his salvation from brokenness?

Man's Possibilities

Although man's relationship with God is broken and he is bio-chemically and interpersonally bound, *his relationship with God may be restored*. This is man's ultimate possibility. The linkage between psychic life and religious restoration consists, in part, in unconscious mental processes. Anxiety, which incipiently is largely beyond awareness, may serve the restoration as well as the breaking of relationship with God. Anxiety may move us toward as well as away from God. The same psychic stuff may be involved in compounding man's plight or actualizing his potentialities in relation to God. *The decisive issue is the presence or absence of repentance and faith.*

Consider again the case of Mr. Mills. In the closing section of the conversation, he is asking the question which Nicodemus put to Jesus. "How can a man be born when he is old?" (John 3:4). Mr.

Mills says, "I am getting along in years though, so I imagine that is the way I will always be" (P.21). Again, "I'm getting old and set in my ways now, and I don't know if I could change" (P.22).

Mr. Mills is asking what possibilities still exist in relation to God? Most of life's possibilities have been exhausted for him. Few possibilities remain in relation to marriage and family life, employment and economic productivity. In terms of health, the possibilities of disease and death are more real than those of sustained health and prolonged life. Intrapsychic and interpersonal structures are firmly set.

Gradually, Mr. Mills is laid hold of by the possibility of restored relationship with God. In considering this possibility, a feeling of wonder grows in him. The feeling of wonder and of hope is not unmixed. Doubt and despair continue to assail him. But wonder and hope confirm the possibility toward which they point. For to hope that religious feeling is still a possibility for one is to experience religious feeling as a reality in one—the feeling of hope.

The presence of a religious feeling such as hope does not necessarily prepare the way for divine-human encounter, however. Mr. Mills' experience is instructive in demonstrating that simple equations between bondage and brokenness and between health and salvation are not adequate. On the basis of clinical observation, we can say that the hope of restored health may prepare the way for the hope of restoration in relation to God, but we cannot say that it necessarily will prepare the way. Furthermore, we cannot say that the despair of health will block the emergence of hope for divine-human encounter. We can say only that linkage exists between amelioration of a person's bondage and the restoration of brokenness in relation to God. We do not know how to describe the linkage. We do not know whether it appears necessarily or arbitrarily, in predictable or random patterns.

David Roberts offers a moving witness to the way in which psychiatric healing may prepare the way for repentance and faith.[5] He has

[5] David E. Roberts, *Psychotherapy and the Christian View of Man* (New York: Charles Scribner's Sons, 1951): Roberts errs in generalizing too widely on the experience of a few persons in psychotherapy. He equates the bondage of neurotic conflicts directly with the brokenness of sin. He equates a relationship of acceptance with the experience of Divine Grace. As I have shown already, this is much too simple to do justice to either clinical or theological data. His work has more merit as a witness than as a dogmatic formulation.

written the story of many ministers who are engaged in clinical pastoral education and of many more persons involved in pastoral counseling and other forms of psychotherapy. Many of us have found, as Roberts did, that irrationality may *"implement* our search for truth and our willingness to act in the light of it" as well as *"prevent* us."[6] Sin—the breaking of relationship with God—is more often found in moralistic self-control than in self-understanding, in avoiding therapeutic relationships rather than in entering them, in the constriction of conscience rather than in its expansion. Sin may take the form of evading responsibility for assimilating the full reality of one's psychic bondage.

Grace—the restoration of relationship with God—often becomes decisive in the context of interpersonal relationships marked by mutual trust and acceptance. Roberts says that an experience of grace in the context of interpersonal acceptance issues in graciousness of spirit in contrast to a legalistic spirit. It stimulates

> wholeheartedness, deep friendship, full experience of both the bodily and the spiritual riches of human love, steady joy in living, the unforced employment of talents . . . and the development of interests which have never been given a chance.[7]

In spite of the fact that many persons experience the realities of sin and salvation in direct relation to intrapsychic discoveries, we do well not to generalize from such testimonies. In some religious communities the predominant testimony is that salvation occurs in the midst of disease, death and depravity. Psychological healing does not appear to be involved in the preparation of the way for salvation, except in an implicit sense. If the possibility for restoration of relationship between God and man does not inhere necessarily in intrapsychic or interpersonal healing, wherein does the possibility inhere?

The Biblical witness is that the possibility for restoration of relationship with God inheres in repentance and faith. Repentance and faith do not occur in isolation but in community. Thus confession within the religious community and commitment to the com-

⁶ *Ibid.,* p. 58.
⁷ *Ibid.,* p. 98.

munity are actions which inhere in the realization of man's ultimate possibility. Discussion of confession and commitment is reserved for the following chapter. Repentance and faith are to be considered here.

My point of view is that repentance and faith are linked both with unconscious and with conscious mental processes. Repentance refers phenomenologically to the disorganization of one's total personality and faith to one's reorganization around a new center of loyalty. Repentance is significantly linked with the simultaneous feeling of despair and hope in relation to God. Faith is associated with the perception of personal meaning in the events of history and nature; it is the pursuit of truth in subjectivity. It is, as H. Richard Niebuhr says, the perception of one's "own history" and commitment to the community in which one's own history is unfolded. Thus faith is less concerned with what is believed, sensed, conceived than with the process of knowing, feeling and willing.[8]

Repentance and faith describe one's movement from observing and reflecting upon religious history in terms of the -eds (what is believed, for instance) to participation in the history of a religious community in terms of the -ings (the process of believing, confessing and committing one's self).[9] This movement is neither developmentally determined nor rationally comprehensible. The rational constructs involved in Christian commitment are logically absurd—that the Word became flesh, for example. Repentance and faith require what Kierkegaard calls "the leap," and this is accomplished in irrationality.

The presence of both despair and hope in repentance is seen in the preaching of John the Baptist (Matthew 3:1-12). John warned his contemporaries of wrath to come and of fiery judgment. In requiring baptism of the Jews, he said, in effect, you are no better than the heathen and you must begin all over again. Your heritage as heirs of Abraham affords you no immunity from divine judgment. John's word of judgment inheres in his word of hope, however. He came preaching, "Repent, for *the kingdom of heaven is at hand*" [italics mine] (Matthew 3:2). In him who will baptize with the Holy Spirit is the people's hope and in him is their dread:

[8] H. Richard Niebuhr, *The Meaning of Revelation* (New York: The Macmillan Company, 1962), pp. 64-65.
[9] *Ibid.*, pp. 83-84.

His winnowing fork is in his hand, and he will clean his threshing floor and gather his wheat into the granary, but the chaff he will burn with unquenchable fire (Matthew 3:12).

The Coming One will perceive men's motives; he will accept only those who are spiritual heirs of Abraham. As Abraham offered Isaac, so the repentant one must relinquish his reliance upon external, objective history; he must be driven inward to an examination of his internal, subjective history. He must experience the meaning of being a self-before-God. He must know himself naked and exposed and without defense before God.

It is inwardness, then, that triggers the sense of judgment. John the Baptist did not call for repentance in response to an externally imposed judgment. He spoke to an audience who came out to him. They came trusting his integrity and were already prepared for the confrontation of judgment, because they came to hear his proclamation of the Messiah. The hope of Messiah judged the false hopes by which the people lived. The repentance, for which the prophet called, was a turning from illusion to truth, from the false hope based on Israel's external history to a true hope based on the prophetic community's discovery of the possibility of a new internal history.

Man's ultimate possibility is the possibility of a leap of faith from trust in illusion to trust in the living God to whom witness is given in the community of faith. Man's most fulfilling possibility is not a new or more exact body of knowledge but a new way of knowing, not the chronological extension of life but the qualitative transformation of one's living, not in rational comprehension of theology but in irrational commitment to the Lord of a confessing community.

Jesus added to John's message the theme: "believe in the gospel" (Mark 1:15). Actually repentance and faith are inseparable. Each is implicit in the other. Without already believing in the possibility of salvation, a man cannot bear the threat to his self-esteem that repentance implies. Inward awareness that one's values are illusory evokes acute anxiety. This may be constructive—leading to salvation; but it may be destructive—resulting in a hardening and a shriveling of one's capacity to respond to God. The apostle Paul recognized the concurrence of both possibility and plight in the psychic phenomenon of repentance:

godly grief produces a repentance that leads to salvation and brings
no regret, but worldly grief produces death (2 Corinthians 7:10).

Thus the conditions that make possible a leap of faith make possible
also a drawing back in unbelief—an ultimately tragic loss of relationship with God. An explication of repentance and faith discloses
not only new heights of human possibility but also new depths of the
human plight.

The conversion of St. Augustine illustrates unconscious processes
in repentance and the irrational nature of the leap from plight to
possibility in relationship to God. In *The Confessions of Saint Augustine* we see hints of the linkage between neurotic bondage and
spiritual brokenness. The interpenetration of human forms of
ministry and of Divine Grace is suggested, too.

At age 29, Augustine suffered a critical illness. He was in conflict
with his Christian mother, Monica, over his Manichaeanism. His
illness and the threatened loss of approval from his religiously zealous
mother radically disorganized Augustine's self concept. His anxiety
shifted masks—from proud self-sufficiency to feelings of futility and
a fear of finitude. As a teacher of rhetoric in Milan, he sought out
the Catholic Bishop, Ambrose, because of the Bishop's fame as a
rhetorician. From his first meeting, he began "to love him" and to
open his heart to him—admitting only how eloquently he spoke at
first, but gradually admitting how truly he spoke. From this time
until his thirty-second year, Augustine says, "and yet was I drawing
nearer by little and little, and *unconsciously*" [italics mine].[10]

Augustine's thirtieth birthday was significant in the process of his
repentance. Characteristically, the decade turning points are anxiety
provoking to adults. He acknowledged that he was far from his
coveted goal of finding wisdom; he saw himself "sticking in the
same mire, greedy of enjoying things present, which passed away
and wasted my soul." He took comfort in the thought, "Tomorrow
I shall find it [wisdom] . . . lo, Faustus the Manichee will come,
and clear every thing!" In this passage, Augustine confesses his
transference of the wish to be omniscient to the famous scholar,
Faustus.[11]

[10] Edward B. Pussey, trans., *The Confessions of Saint Augustine* (New
York: The Modern Library, 1949), pp. 92–93.
[11] *Ibid.*, p. 111.

Dependence, passivity and irresponsible indulgence of his sexual needs appear in his confessions soon thereafter. With his chum, Alypius, he fought against his mother's efforts to have him married. Instead he lived with Alypius and enjoyed his concubine, having a son by her. When she was taken from him on the occasion of his engagement, he procured another woman. He notes that his anxiety "became less acute, but more desperate."[12]

The leap of faith occurred after a 3-year-period of unconscious incubation. The final sequence of events is well known. Augustine talked with a Christian pastor, Simplicianus, the successor of Ambrose in Milan. Simplicianus allowed him to ventilate his anxieties and then shared with him the story of Victorinus, a Roman scholar and rhetorician who gave up his status in Roman aristocratic society to publicly confess himself a Christian. Augustine felt immediately "on fire to imitate him." He found, however, that

> the new will which had begun to be in me, freely to serve Thee
> . . . was not yet able to overcome my former wilfulness, strength-
> ened by age. Thus did my two wills, one new, and the other old,
> one carnal, the other spiritual, struggle within me; and by their
> discord undid my soul.[13]

Augustine reports next that in his efforts to meditate on the things of God he was "overcome with a heavy drowsiness."[14] This is an interesting clinical description of selective inattention.

Finally, the inner conflict broke out again. In a moment of acute psychic anguish, Augustine heard a child say to a playmate: "Take up and read; take up and read." He found the Scriptures and read:

> Not in rioting and drunkenness, not in chambering and wantonness,
> not in strife and envying; but put ye on the Lord Jesus Christ, and
> make no provision for the flesh, in concupiscence.[15]

In this moment, Augustine made the leap of faith, which means wholehearted commitment to God and to the Christian community. When his conversation became articulated in theological terminol-

12 *Ibid.*, p. 116.
13 *Ibid.*, pp. 152–153.
14 *Ibid.*, p. 153.
15 *Ibid.*, p. 167.

ogy many years later, Augustine attributed the entire process of repentance and the leap of faith to the absolute, primary, unconscious activity of Divine Grace—prevenient, operative, irresistible and cooperating.

Augustine's conversion demonstrates the complexity of the processes of repentance and faith. It suggests a sizeable period of time and the juxtaposition of diverse persons and forces—both conscious and unconscious—in the life of one individual. Parental and developmental factors are deeply interwoven in the fabric of Augustine's religious experience. Chronic conflict between Monica and her husband over their son's education and religious affiliation was a major factor. A critical illness and a thirtieth birthday focused his attention on the psychic realities of middle adulthood. The role of Christian pastors, though secondary, was not without significance, however.

The way was prepared for divine-human encounter by Ambrose and Simplicianus. Ambrose offered Augustine a relationship "not as a teacher of the truth (which I utterly despaired of in Thy Church), but as a person kind towards myself."[16] Simplicianus, like Ambrose, gave Augustine a warm, personal relationship. He listened to him. He participated in Augustine's defiance and doubt, trusting this to prepare further the way for repentance and faith. To be sure, both Ambrose and Simplicianus also proclaimed the Word of the gospel— Ambrose in sermon and Simplicianus in story. Neither participation nor proclamation is adequate alone.

The exhortation of Simplicianus both judged and inspired Augustine. The pastor activated Augustine's inner conflicts but then failed to help him resolve the conflicts. I will speculate that a more skilled pastoral counselor might have made the way for God's coming more "straight." Deeper participation in the conflict might have speeded the coming of the decisive moment before God. In no sense does pastoral counseling bypass the necessity for a leap of faith. One of the risks inherent in counseling is that a spiritually dense pastor may presume to manipulate Divine Grace. He may be inattentive to the necessity for a leap of faith. The limit of pastoral responsibility is to prepare the way for a leap of faith. What, then, does this mean in terms of pastoral functioning?

16 *Ibid.*, p. 92.

Pastoral Participation

The irony of pastoral ministry is that the pastor is caught in the same plight as those whom he would help. He, too, is driven by the need to protect and enhance his self-esteem. He, too, is anxious in the face of the other person who is immediately present in the relationship. The pastor may avoid becoming involved with his parishioner lest he experience himself judged inadequate and accepted in spite of his inadequacies. In either case the pastor, like his parishioner, is subject to divine encounter in the context of counseling. Each may focus on the past or the future, on regrets and hopes, on resentments and fears, on beliefs and promises rather than on the present reality—the reality of interpersonal and of divine-human encounter.

One may prepare the way for repentance and faith as one participates in the process of psychic discovery. Participation means that the pastor remains open both to the full reality of his parishioner's plight and to new dimensions of his own plight. Pastoral participation aims at relief of psychic distress but is attentive to the interpenetration of bondage and brokenness in relation to God. Repentance and the leap of faith describe subjective realities. The Holy Spirit is the name of God as he is known in subjectivity. The pastor can neither predict nor control the occurrence of repentance and faith; he cannot manipulate the activity of the Holy Spirit. Through participation in the psychic life of his people and openness to his own psychic reality, however, a pastor may be given the opportunity to "prepare the way of the Lord" (Matthew 3:3).

CHAPTER SEVEN

PREPARE *The* WAY *For* COMMITMENT

The leap of faith (as defined in Chapter Six) means commitment to a community of faith. It is more than a leap into a new way of thinking; it is a leap into a new way of living. It is more than commitment to a particular system of belief; it is commitment to a particular community—a community created and sustained by a common center of faith. Commitment is inconceivable apart from community. Community implies a common center of faith.

What has pastoral care and counseling to do with commitment? If commitment requires a community of faith as its context and goal, how may pastoral counseling prepare the way? Pastoral care and counseling customarily implies a one-to-one relationship of pastor and parishioner. Contemporary pastoral counseling has been built on a medical model. According to this model, the expert professional man ministers to a succession of individuals with little attention to the community context in which they live. With the appearance of the pastoral counseling center as a significant new form of pastoral ministry, little effort is made to relate pastoral counseling to a religious community in an integral way.[1] The context of ministry may include an intake interview, setting of fees, referral for psychological testing or psychiatric consultation and tape recording of interviews, but not public worship or instruction in theology. The locus of ministry is often a clinic-type building. The relationship of such counseling to the church as a community is usually tangential at best. Administrative connections afford the counselor some identity as a representative of a religious community. He functions outside the context of a local congregation or parish in most instances.

The concept of Christian community calls for a reappraisal of pastoral counseling, and I shall give attention to this in the next

[1] James N. Lapsley, Jr., "Pastoral Counseling Centers: Mid-Century Phenomenon," *Pastoral Psychology*, XIII, No. 130 (1963), pp. 43–52.

chapter. My primary focus throughout this book is on the psychic rather than the social aspects of religious experience. Before looking at pastoral counseling from the perspective of community, therefore, I shall ask whether pastoral counseling may prepare the way for commitment in terms of intrapsychic preparation.

To concretize the discussion, I shall present a clinical example involving commitment to a religious vocation. Next, the intrapsychic aspects of commitment will be considered in relation to Jung's psychoanalytic concept of individuation. Finally, in Chapter Eight, I shall take a theological perspective and develop the theme of commitment to a community of faith.

Commitment to Vocation: A Clinical Study

Commitment to a church-related vocation is linked with the pressure of unconscious forces upon consciousness. Some clues as to the nature of this linkage are found in the experience of a minister whom I shall call Bill Forrester. Bill is a 30-year-old minister who is married and the father of several children. On referral from an official of his denomination's foreign mission society he entered counseling to increase his readiness for appointment. On the basis of a psychiatric examination, he had been postponed. In counseling, the following picture emerged.

Bill publicly confessed a call to the ministry at the age of 19. He says, "God had been calling me to preach the gospel for some time, but I had not been willing to face it." After accepting the call, he reports, "I had great joy in my heart because I knew that I was in the center of God's will for me."

Eleven years later he presents himself in counseling as a benign but ineffective person. He is insecure and anxious. He has not established his independence from his parents, particularly from his mother. His wife has a similar problem in relation to her mother, who lives in the home. Bill and his wife want to become foreign missionaries. Their motivation is partially derived from a desire to escape the problems created by his mother-in-law. Bill suffers severe headaches, which medical diagnosis has found to be functional.

Bill is a colorless person. He gives no outward evidence of undue hostility or other dark emotions. He is so severely repressed that he appears shallow and superficial. He reports a strong dislike for discord and confusion and he avoids the stresses of interpersonal relationships in several ways. Avoidance patterns include illness, shifting of administrative responsibilities in the church to his wife, excessive compliance with the expectations of church members and excessive self-depreciation. These maneuvers protect him from direct interaction with others and reduce the risk of disapproval. He has a few special techniques of avoidance. He often drives into the country to secluded wooded spots for prayer and meditation. He spends excessive blocks of time in these hideaways. He bought half interest in an airplane and learned to fly. Flying is justified as a remedy for his headaches.

In the role of minister, Bill is passive and unimaginative. He finds sermon preparation a heavy and unrewarding chore. His headaches become worse during sermon preparation, and he constantly interrupts his study schedule to fly his plane. Ostensibly he is clearing his head for further study. Church administration is delegated almost entirely to his wife. She has been employed as church secretary and choir director. She coordinated the last financial drive to underwrite the church budget. Pastoral calling is done on demand only and in a perfunctory way. Bill's time is exploited by the more demanding members of his congregation. Because of unrecognized resentment, he does as little pastoral calling as possible.

Bill was seen in counseling ten times. After an interval of nearly 6 months, he returned for a sequence of three additional conferences. My counseling procedure was to focus initially upon his motivation for and resistance to counseling. Then, as he became secure in the relationship and when some longings for healing became conscious, I helped him to experience himself more and more fully in a feeling way. The dark and shadowy dimension of his life experience was gradually assimilated into conscious awareness.

As Bill returns for the second round of counseling conferences, he is changed in several respects. He looks me in the eye and presents himself with emotional strength. His manner and tone of voice reveal that he is possessed of a deep calm which is characteristic of those who experience a marked degree of emotional integration or wholeness of heart.

By this time he has identified and assimilated the major traumata of his childhood experience. He is aware of most of the ways in which he manipulates his feelings and behavior to maintain the image of a son beloved of his mother. He is already emotionally weaned from his parents. He and his wife have realistically solved the problems arising from the presence of the mother-in-law in the home.

Bill is able to laugh about his prior need to avoid people by rituals of driving to lonely rural hideaways or flying his plane. He mentions, incidentally, that he has sold his interest in the plane. He now finds Bible study absorbing and rewarding.

Freedom to face and assimilate old patterns of avoidance is reflected in new behavior as a minister. He is finding the strength within himself to meet his parishioners directly—including his critics and would-be manipulators. He has encouraged his wife to resign as church secretary, and he is taking responsibility himself for the administration of the church program. He has begun an intensive program of ministry in the local hospital. He has won the support of the nursing staff and of some of the doctors in the community for his new style of pastoral ministry. One doctor has remained cool and aloof. Bill says that the problem in their relationship is more in the doctor than in himself. Whether his evaluation of the situation is right or wrong, it is significant that he does not react intrapunitively to this doctor's rejection of him, that is, he does not take responsibility entirely upon himself. In all of these relationships, he is demonstrating a previously lacking capacity for objectivity in relationships.

Bible study is taking on new meaning for Bill. He is deeply immersed in a re-study of Christ's pastoral ministry. He sees contradictions between the Biblical record and traditional types of programing used in the churches of his denomination. In the face of strong pressure from his fellow pastors to conform, he has adapted a denominational program to the specific needs of his own congregation. He is affirming himself to be free of excessive needs for their approval. He does this not in a negativistic and self-defeating way, but in a way appropriate to the best interests of his congregation.

In the midst of his counseling pilgrimage, what happened to Bill's sense of commitment to the ministry? He put it this way: "I can honestly say that I am no longer consumed with the question of whether or not we will be appointed for mission service. I know now that I have a ministry and that I can perform it with real significance for others wherever I am. I would be satisfied to spend the rest of my life here in the States if we are not appointed. I don't have to go to the other side of the globe to feel that my ministry is significant. I feel that significance is not determined by the geography on which I stand, but by the quality of relationships in which I live with those around me. I guess you could say that *I am possessed of a new purpose for being in the ministry.*"

A few months later Bill had a second psychiatric evaluation. He was given a clean bill of health both medically and emotionally. He received enthusiastic endorsement from the same psychiatrist who 18 months before had found him definitely not recommendable from a psychiatric point of view.

In Bill's experience we discover wide diversity in the psychological meaning of his vocational commitment. The meaning of his commitment at age 19 is at one end of a continuum and his post-counseling commitment at age 30 is at the other end. Bill described his early experience as being "called" into the ministry; his later experience he described as being "possessed" by a new purpose for ministry. I shall use his own terms, "called" and "possessed," as a shorthand reference to this continuum. Then I shall compare and contrast these two manifestations of commitment from a psychological perspective.

Commitment to the ministry may serve to deny to awareness the shadowy, unconscious aspects of one's experience; in contrast, commitment to ministry may be a response to the assimilation of the unconscious aspects of one's experience. The denial of one's shadows marks the experience of being "called," and response to one's shadows issues in an experience of being "possessed." Being "called" into ministry is experienced as a response to God, who is felt to be largely external to one's self; in being "possessed," God is experienced as internal or within one's self. Being "called" characteristically occurs in the teens or early twenties; being "possessed" usually occurs in the second half of life—from the thirties on. The experience of being "called" into ministry is linked with the developmental process of identification with the adult community. One is focused on a particular vocational slot within the organized religious community. When one is "possessed" for ministry, he measures effectiveness not by the plumb line of his office but by the quality of his interpersonal relationships. This experience is linked developmentally with the shift from mastering the external environment to exploring and enjoying one's internal and interpersonal environment. It is associated with the contrast between rational and intuitive knowledge, or, in Martin Buber's terms, the contrast between I-It and I-Thou relationships.

The experience of being "called" increases one's control over erotic and hostile impulses. It compensates for feelings of insignificance and of interpersonal loneliness. The experience of being "called" is used by many persons to reinforce a denial of the tragic and ironic dimensions of human experience. It is associated with striving for moral perfection, nurturing hope of changing the world and denying one's tragic interdependence. At this stage persons tend to be inattentive to the fact that one's virtues may be both a blessing and a curse to those who matter most.

The experience of being "possessed" by a new purpose for ministry follows increased assimilation of previously unconscious experience into consciousness. It is one manifestation of the integration of the dark and shadowy aspects of emotional life into the light of awareness. Being "possessed" is an experience attending the acceptance of one's self as finite. It is related to a growing capacity to tolerate the paradoxical tensions of life. One has begun to relinquish hope for moral perfection and fame. In the midst of this acceptance of imperfection, insignificance and bondage, one experiences himself accepted by God.

The interpersonal relationships of those at the stage of being "called" into ministry are marked by superficiality, manipulativeness or withdrawal. Behavior is often highly compulsive and relieved by little true recreation. The experience of being "called" frequently reinforces one's motivation for higher education and other forms of increasing one's influence upon others. One gradually gains increasing degrees of leadership and, consequently, of power over others.

Manifestations of being "possessed" are increasing spontaneity, emotional honesty and the capacity for depth relationships with people holding widely diverse value systems. One becomes more open and sharing of himself, more attentive to and empathetic with others, more effective in ministry. Behavior becomes markedly less compulsive and more flexible. One is more free to enjoy relationships with others for their own sakes. One becomes less stereotyped and conventional, more creative. Self-derogatory feelings give place to self-affirmation. One's needs for the approval of others diminish in proportion as one gains capacity to sustain deep relationships in a context of emotional honesty.

One's leadership and power over others continues to increase, but one is less dependent upon the external symbols of his office and more confident of his inherent gifts. One's total life experience is caught up in a sense of being "possessed" by a new purpose. Ministry becomes more unified. Organized forms of religion frequently become less important as a means for serving God in the world. As one's service for God becomes less bound by convention, it is experienced to be more relevant to the needs of others. As one becomes increasingly whole, he becomes increasingly sensitive to the emotional needs of others.

By now, it is clear that the experience of being "called," as defined in relation to Bill's pilgrimage, is inextricably interwoven with neurotic patterns of self-protection. The experience of being "possessed" is relatively free from neurotic bondage. Does this mean that the difference between an experience of being "called" to ministry and of being "possessed" by new purpose for ministry is nothing more than the difference between being neurotically bound and being free of neurosis? Do our clinical data tell us anything more than the obvious, that is that all clergymen are more adequate when they are free of neurosis? In my opinion we do see more than the obvious.

We see at least three things: (1) The normal process of development exercises a continuous pressure upon one to integrate the dark and shadowy aspects of experience into the light of awareness. (2) A person who decides to assimilate previously unacceptable thoughts and feelings gains increased capacity to commit himself to a community of faith. The process of assimilation is effected by means of voluntary decision; it does not occur automatically. (3) Pastoral counseling or psychotherapy prepares the way for commitment insofar as it helps a person to decide for psychic wholeness. In a sense, everyone who seriously follows through in counseling has already decided in favor of psychic wholeness; a decision for counseling is necessarily a decision to risk the assimilation of unconscious feelings into consciousness.

Psychic wholeness means increased capacity for commitment, but obviously the community of faith to which one commits himself is not determined within the counseling process. Given a prior commitment to the Christian community, counseling prepares the way for renewing and enhancing this commitment. Bill Forrester illustrates this. Lacking a prior commitment, counseling prepares the way for an initial commitment—a commitment in the mood of ultimate concern, hence, a religious commitment. Jung's concept of individuation illustrates this. The religious meaning of commitment may or may not reflect the counselor's personal loyalties. Here again we see that counseling does not manipulate divine-human encounter, but it prepares the way.

Jung's Concept of Individuation

The above principles are described with precision by the late Carl G. Jung, noted Swiss psychoanalyst. In contrast to Freud, his early teacher and colleague, Jung perceived creative potentialities in man's unconscious life. He saw in adult experience the possibility of what he called individuation. Individuation is a process by which unconscious aspects of man's psychic life are assimilated into consciousness, culminating in an essentially religious experience of vocation.

Jung postulates a supraordinate self in man which encompasses both a personal and a collective unconscious. The ego is the center of consciousness, but the ego is sealed off from most of the stimuli in the outside world and from much of the depth of the subjective world by the persona. Persona is one's shell. It is the mask one wears in public and also the mask one wears in private to shield one from the realities of his unconscious life. It is fluid and adaptable in healthy persons; it is stiff and automatic—like a grown-on mask—in unhealthy persons. One's office or title or one's idealized self often becomes the persona behind which one hides. Behind a stiff persona a person shrivels and shrinks, becoming quite small and empty.

During the first half of life a person must take root in the objective world. He is pressed to cultivate his persona to protect himself from external dangers and to achieve a marketable identity in terms of family, work and society. In the second half of life, man's supraordinate self exerts insistent pressure upon the ego to become open to the subjective world. The subjective world consists of several polarities. The polarity of extroversion-introversion is the best known of Jung's concepts. Jung also describes the polarities of thought and feeling, of sensation and intuition, and others which I shall discuss subsequently. When an adult decides for psychotherapy, a predictable process is set in motion. This process Jung calls individuation or self-realization.

Individuation occurs in response to *pistis,* by which Jung means trustful loyalty to one's inner being.[2] *Pistis* is translated "faith" in the New Testament. For Jung, this is the deciding, choosing factor; it is man's decision to give faithful obedience to his intuitive leadings. These intuitive leadings are crucial in the emergence of personality.[3] Given a commitment in *pistis* to psychotherapy, the process of individuation unfolds. It is slow and full of psychic pain, but it leads inevitably to an experience of vocation.

The first stage is the experience of the shadow. This is called the darker brother of personality. By it Jung means unconscious mental processes. Jung says that no progress on the way to wholeness can be made until one becomes conscious of the shadowy depths of one's own nature, accepts its reality and remains always aware of its reality as part of his being.

The second stage on the road to vocation is marked by meeting one's soul-image. The soul-image is the image of the opposite sex which each one carries within himself. It is man's Eve and woman's Adam. The soul-image of a so-called intellectual person is sentimentality. In the apparently sentimental person, the soul-image is coldly analytical. Every man, no matter how self-disciplined and authoritative, bears within himself feminine drives and intuitions. Every woman, no matter how irrational she may appear, bears within her the rationality which we associate with masculinity. Discovery of this contrasexuality within one's self is an unmistakable sign that the second half of life has begun. It is the necessary precondition to fruitful adult living.

Jung finds the third phase of the process of individuation to be the appearance of the old wise man. This he describes as the discovery that the essence of life is spiritual and not material. It entails

[2] Carl G. Jung, *The Development of Personality,* trans. R. F. C. Hull, Volume 17, Bollingen Series XX. Copyright, 1954 by Bollingen Foundation, Inc., New York. Published for Bollingen Foundation, Inc. by Pantheon Books Inc., New York, pp. 174–186.

[3] Carl G. Jung, *Psychology and Alchemy,* Volume 12, Bollingen Series XX. Copyright, 1953 by Bollingen Foundation, Inc., New York. Published for Bollingen Foundation, Inc. by Pantheon Books Inc., New York, p. 13.

the recognition of one's finitude, the acceptance of shrinking areas of freedom. This is liberation from materialistic goals. It is freedom from bondage to human ties, such as an ultimate loyalty to one's clan, church, nation or race.

The fourth phase of one's individuation is the experience of vocation. One comes to the point at which he discovers his self. In this sense the process may be called self-realization. The self is defined by Jung as "the aim of life." The self becomes for one what Meister Eckhart called our "central fire." Vocation is defined literally: "to be addressed by a voice." This is, for Jung, a decisive moment. It comes with the driving force of a compulsion; it carries the sense of predestination. It is experienced as objectively real though psychic in form. It is heavy as lead, hard and real as iron.[4]

Jung says that vocation is experienced first as a negative voice—as temptation to evil. I think at once of Jesus' temptations. The voice of God led Jesus into the wilderness region, and the voice of God addressed Jesus after he had been addressed by the devil. Jung says of the negative voice or the temptation to evil:

> If we do not partially succumb, nothing of this apparent evil enters into us, and no regeneration or healing can take place. . . . If we succumb completely, then the contents expressed by the inner voice act as so many devils, and a catastrophe ensues. But if we can succumb only in part, and if by self-assertion the ego can save itself from being completely swallowed, then it can assimilate the voice, and we realize that the evil was, after all, only a semblance of evil, but in reality a bringer of healing and illumination.[5]

Vocation, then, brings with it a sense of new birth, of illumination, of healing and of freedom. One is freed from the bondage of the traditional and from the mass man. One is freed from the unconsciousness of vocation which lulls most people. In this connection, Jung says that neurotic states are defenses against the dim awareness of vocation in one's psychic depths. "Behind the neurotic perversion is concealed his vocation, his destiny: the growth of personality, the full realization of the life-will that is born with the individual."[6]

---

[4] Jung, *The Development of Personality*, pp. 174–185.
[5] *Ibid.*, p. 185.
[6] *Ibid.*

In this sketch of Jung's concept of individuation we see substantial empirical evidence that the psychic processes implicit in successful counseling and psychotherapy prepare the way for commitment. The content of commitment is not defined by psychic readiness "to be addressed by a voice" or to be "possessed" by a new purpose, however. For this reason a pastoral counselor must not stop at this point. We need to take a serious look at counseling and commitment from a theological perspective—the perspective of the church or the community of faith.

CHAPTER EIGHT

PREPARE The WAY For A
COMMUNITY Of FAITH

Togetherness was not the chief goal of the early Christian fellowship. The mutual sharing of burdens and confession of sins was explicitly related to a primary commitment of the entire community to God. Christian community is built on the confession first spoken by Simon Peter, "You are the Christ, the Son of the living God" (Matthew 16:16). The Biblical record bears witness to the fact that the early Christian community found its cohesiveness in common commitment to Jesus Christ. *Koinonia*, the Biblical word for fellowship, connotes commitment to God as the original and primary bond and commitment to one another, or the mutual care of souls, as a derived and secondary bond of fellowship.

The leap of faith by which one makes his initial commitment to the Christian community is understood within the community to be a gift of the Holy Spirit. The deepening of commitment described in the case of the Rev. Bill Forrester reflects the work of the Holy Spirit as well. Wayne E. Oates aptly says, "the primary mode of encounter of the individual self by the Holy Spirit is *in relation to the Christian community*.[1] We see here a reciprocal movement between commitment and community. Commitment to Christian community is primarily a commitment to God, yet commitment to God is essentially commitment to the Christian community. Because of their interpenetration, we must consider them together. I shall review some of the characteristics of Christian community and note the function of pastoral counseling in preparing the way for commitment to a community of faith.

[1] Oates, *Christ and Selfhood*, p. 147.

The Celebrative Use of Conflict

Christian community is built on the celebrative use of conflict. I use the word celebrative deliberately rather than the more familiar phrase: the creative use of conflict. The celebrative use of conflict is creative, but it connotes more than this. Celebrative is used with the meaning implicit in celebrating the atoning death of Christ in the Communion. The Communion reminds us that God transformed the tragedy of Christ's death into resurrection; God transformed one community's vicious hatred into a new community that knew no law save this: "that you love one another" (John 15:12). The Communion anticipates the consummation of Christian community in which all the barriers of sect, race, sex and time are overcome. The divine initiative that created a new community in the past and that will bring Christian community to consummation in the future is worthy of celebration. Likewise the Holy Spirit takes initiative to create Christian community in the midst of present conflict, thereby evoking our celebration of God's grace in the midst of our present existence.

The celebrative use of conflict is a bold wrestling with conflict in the confidence that it, like the angel with whom Jacob wrestled, will give us a blessing. Christian community grows best where people believe that conflict is not an alien force in the life of the community but is an evidence of the presence of the Holy Spirit re-forming the goals and refining the motivations of the community. Strange as it seems, Christian community may thrive on hostile encounters between persons who hold contradictory opinions. Assuming that all parties to the conflict are deeply confident that they *belong* to the community, hostile encounter often is the *sine qua non* of genuine fellowship. Failure of nerve at the point of challenge is in reality a failure of the will-for-community with one's antagonist. If I avoid conflict with someone or some group within my community, I may in fact betray my commitment to the community.

Pastoral counseling equips individuals for the celebrative use of conflict within their respective communities by liberating them for emotional honesty. The counseling process stimulates spontaneous expression of both tender and hostile feelings. In Christian community the taboo against anger is the major block to depth of commitment. The paradox that true love is nourished by honestly expressed hostility is illustrated in a premarital counseling process. On the first visit, both the prospective bride and groom related with pride that they had not had a single quarrel during their courtship. I commented, "Your love must be quite fragile if you have not been able honestly to explore your differences." In the second session a week later, the couple reported that they began to quarrel soon after leaving my office and had quarreled often during the week. What emerged were gross conflicts of value, which had previously been avoided because of the desperate need of each for the feeling that he had found a perfect love. The young man soon confessed that he had been previously married and that the divorce was not yet final. His fiancée communicated her resentment openly. Each saw how phony their "perfect" love had been. After several months of counseling and after painstaking repair of the broken covenant, they were married. The marriage ceremony was just another celebration of nuptials to most of those who attended. To the couple and to me it was also the celebration of the grace of God made manifest in the midst of conflict. Whether in premarital or marital conflict, the honest communication of negative feelings opens the door for reconciliation, provided, of course, the basic integrity of a couple's covenant with each other has not been broken past repair.

In church life the open communication of negative feelings is highly taboo. I believe that the primary reason for this is that most church members do not feel deeply committed to the community in which they hold membership. The fear of emotional honesty in many church members is a sad witness to the shallowness of the bonds of fellowship. Back-biting, passive resistance to the program of the church and neglect of one's duties usually express greater superficiality in commitment than active opposition to the church programs and direct encounter of leadership in hostile debate of the issues.

The greatest single need of most pastors in relation to church administration is for the freedom to be emotionally honest with both themselves and the lay leadership of their churches. This freedom is born of faith in the celebrative use of conflict. The problem is seen concretely in the case of a pastor who referred his secretary, Mrs. Myrtle Case, to me for pastoral counseling. Mrs. Case was a middle-aged woman struggling to save her marriage. Her husband was infatuated with a widow who, prior to the death of her mate, had been on a best-friend basis with the Case family. As counselor I saw Mrs. Case within the field of interfamilial interaction. I did not see her within the field of the Christian community.

A few months later I became interim pastor of the congregation for which Mrs. Case was church secretary. The counseling problem immediately took a different shape. I discovered that the widow in whom Mr. Case was interested was a prominent lay leader of the congregation. Mr. Case was also regarded as a leader. The entire congregation, which numbered three or four hundred people, knew about the triangle and made it a topic of regular conversation. The former pastor, who referred Mrs. Case for counseling, had adopted an ostrich approach to the problem. Threatened by the possibility of conflict within the congregation and severely limited in his ability to be emotionally honest with himself and others, this pastor avoided both the interpersonal and the administrative aspects of the problem. The official board of the church looked to the pastor to help them find some way to deal with the problem, inasmuch as all three persons in the triangle were church leaders. The pastor avoided facing the issue with them, however. The young people of the church were self-righteously hostile toward the adults for tolerating what they felt was a scandal, and they were especially disillusioned by the passivity of their former pastor.

I responded to the problem by talking individually with members of the official board to ascertain their attitudes not only toward the persons in question but also toward the responsibility of the board for church discipline. The subject was next discussed in a board meeting. I helped the men to discriminate between punitive and pastoral goals in church discipline but left to them the responsibility of making specific recommendations. The members of the board found that some of their number already had good communication with the two families. Responsibility was delegated to a small committee to talk with the widow and Mr. Case and to communicate two feelings: (1) the confidence of the board in the Christian integrity of the persons, and (2) the concern of the board that the presumption of scandal had in fact scandalized the young people of the church. No administrative decision relative to the offices which these persons held in the church was made at this stage. I offered to accompany the laymen on their mission of confrontation, but they felt adequate to the task and did not feel that I needed to become directly identified with their exercise of pastoral discipline.

Soon after the visit from the board representatives, the widow announced her decision to move to another state. The Case couple resolved their chronic marital conflict by divorce. Later, I was told that Mr. Case moved away also and married the widow the following year.

Problems of this kind do not yield to ideal solutions. The board of the church felt, however, that the resolution described was cause for a time of prayer celebrating the Providence which saved the church from scandal and, simultaneously, saved the persons who created the offense from feeling rejected by the Christian community. At no point did the persons involved in the triangle doubt the underlying good will and trust of the board members toward them. I confessed to the laymen who gave leadership in this matter that it was in fear and trembling that I opened the issue with them. I do not know whether or not I would have done so had I been financially dependent on the congregation. This episode increased my faith, however, in the celebrative value of conflict and reinforced my conviction that a pastor's major need in dealing with problems of church discipline is for the emotional freedom necessary to face up to negative feelings that are potentially destructive of the community.

Testing the Spirits

A second requirement of Christian community is a capacity among its members to make discriminating judgments concerning the spirit of would-be leaders. A cogent discussion of this theme is found in 1 John 4. The passage begins, "Beloved, do not believe every spirit, but test the spirits to see whether they are of God" (1 John 4:1). Two tests of the spirits are discussed: (1) the test of *what* one believes and (2) the test of *how* one believes. The test of *what* one believes is stated in this way: "By this you know the Spirit of God: every spirit which does not confess Jesus is not of God" (1 John 4:2–3). The test of *how* one believes is introduced with the words: "Beloved, let us love one another; for love is of God, and he who loves is born of God and knows God. He who does not love does not know God, for God is love" (1 John 4:7–8).

The first test of the spirits is a confession of faith that Jesus Christ has come in the flesh. The epistle was addressed originally to the gnostic heresy. Without doing violence to the passage, we may bypass the particular doctrines of the gnostics and observe that gnosticism rested on the assumption that God can be understood rationally. The gnostics did not question the adequacy of philosophy as philosophy to explain the mysteries of God. The confession that Christ came in the flesh contradicts this gnostic assumption. The confession says, in effect, that God cannot be contained in a system of thought or of dogma. God meets us not logically but absurdly— not in the sophistication of metaphysics but in the scandal of the cross, not in the emanations of Mind but in the incarnation of the Word in human flesh. We know him not in the esoteric knowledge of the gnostics. We know God as we are met by him in the person of Jesus Christ and by the power of the Holy Spirit. To be met by God-in-Christ is to be met and grasped by love, for God is love.

Thus a second and equally indispensable test of the spirits is the test of love. What one believes is important, but the spirit in which one believes is equally important. We separate the *what* from the *how* or the matter from the spirit of belief only at the risk of disruption of fellowship within the Christian community. I recently observed a church bus which bore the slogan, "It *Does* Make a Difference What You Believe!" My response was to say to myself, "Of course it makes a difference what you believe. Beliefs are to a person like eyes. They shape the meaning of the world around us and this in turn shapes behavior. But why advertise the fact?" Knowing the church that owned the bus, I have reason to think that preoccupation with the *what* of their beliefs obscures attention to the spirit in which their beliefs are held. I have known many of its members to manifest a spirit of bitterness, self-righteousness and isolation toward other Christian groups.

The Epistle observes that "there is no fear in love" (1 John 4:18). We do well to reflect on the view that where fear or hate enter, truth departs. Our Lord exercised his ministry among Pharisees who obeyed God fanatically but who obeyed in the spirit of fear and of hate, in closedness of mind and in spiritual pride. They prized the purity of their doctrine but sacrificed purity of heart. Jesus confronted the Pharisees with a clearer view of God, a healthier, more life-giving way; he created a more dedicated community of faith. Then he faced the extinction of both his own life and his cause. Should he fear for his cause? Should he fight for it? He chose the cross because, in my opinion, he knew that to respond to his enemies with fear and hate would be to destroy not only his enemies but also his cause. He suffered and died not only because of *what* he believed, but also because of *how* he believed—because he believed with suffering love.

Pastoral counseling prepares the way for the kind of community in which persons are able to test the spirits with discrimination. Counseling and psychotherapy is by definition a process in which persons test the spirits which move them personally. My own experience as a counselee yielded this result among others. At one point I focused on my failure to effect a reconciliation between factions within the church of which I was pastor. For a year I had preached on variations of the same theme: Love one another! The faction within the church had grown deeper instead of healing. In counseling I discovered that, while I had been preaching on love, I had been preaching *with all the hostility which I could muster*. My congregation was responding to the feeling more than to the content of my messages. And I was confused by my pastoral failure.

Some ability to test the spirits is prerequisite to the celebrative use of conflict. Since I was unable to discern the spirit of hostility which controlled me, I was unable to deal therapeutically with the spirit of hostility which had infected the congregation. Counseling prepares the way for genuine community by heightening our awareness of the emotional dynamics of interpersonal relationships. Pastors who tend to overemphasize the intellectual dimension of life discover in counseling the extent to which the content of belief is shaped by the spirit in which one believes.

Commitment to a Particular Community

A third requirement of Christian community is disciplined dedication to a particular community as the concrete embodiment of Christ in the world. Boisen has shown that commitment to God without disciplined, responsible participation in a community of faith is a form of emotional sickness.[2] Violation of the discipline which creates Christian community was regarded by the early church as a grievous sin. The tragic death of Ananias and Sapphira establishes this point. The original Christian community completely identified the Holy Spirit and the church. Ananias and Sapphira embezzled church funds. The proceeds of the sale of their property presumably had been already dedicated to the community. Their sin, then, was not simply against themselves and their Christian brothers. It was against the church, which meant also the Holy Spirit. Peter said, "Ananias, why has Satan filled your heart to lie to the Holy Spirit? . . . You have not lied to men but to God" (Acts 5:3, 4). It is noteworthy that the word *church* is used here for the first time as a name for the Christian community.[3]

As a Baptist minister, I have had a difficult time accepting the obvious meaning of this episode in the life of the early church. I have tended to minimize the significance of the church as the focus of my loyalty and obedience, while simultaneously affirming the authority of the local church in matters of faith and practice. The import of the Ananias and Sapphira episode is clearly that dedication to Jesus Christ and obedience to the Holy Spirit are inseparable from disciplined dedication to a particular community of faith.

I remember in this connection a dialogue between a Mennonite minister and a group of opponents who represented Lutheran, Methodist and Presbyterian denominations. A few excerpts from the dialogue, which occurred in a student-centered seminar on pastoral theology, will partially define the issues. I shall use G. to designate the Mennonite, because he defined the minister as a representative of God, and C. to designate those who insisted that the minister is a representative of the church.

> C. Are you saying that the reason for your being in the hospital is that you represent the church? This is my view.
>
> G. Actually I don't like this idea of saying that I represent the church. I prefer to say that I am a representative of God. I represent a relationship with God.
>
> C. But there is a covenant community in which this person has his relationship.
>
> G. You go talk to a patient who is facing death and who has never made a decision regarding God. Salvation isn't going to come

[2] Boisen, *The Exploration of the Inner World*, pp. 83–125.
[3] *The Interpreter's Bible*, IX, pp. 75, 78.

through membership in a church but through relationship to God. . . . I shy away from saying that a minister represents the church in the hospital. For me it is more meaningful to say, I represent God-in-Christ. . . . If we say it this way, we see how ministry through relationship becomes pretty significant. If I as a representative of Christ can accept this person with his sins, fears, etc., then by implication the one I represent, God, can accept this person. . . .

C. We can't relate this person to God and leave the church over in the corner if we have a Biblical understanding of what the church is.

G. . . . my view is directly opposed to you. In the last analysis, what is significant is whether I am in relation to God, not whether I am in relationship to the church. . . . I feel this very strongly. . . . in the last analysis my responsibility is to God, not the church.

C. You are a self-appointed ambassador of God?

G. Absolutely not! I've gotten authority from God on the basis of my experience of him. I'm not placing responsibility on myself. . . . I'm not saying the church is not significant. I'm simply saying that Jesus called his followers as individuals—whosoever believeth in me.

C. No, Jesus had the concept of the corporate body in mind. Hebraic man never understood himself as an individual, but as part of the corporate body.

The free church tradition represented by the Mennonite minister minimizes the role of the church in Christian experience in protest against the tendency to substitute human associations for divine-human encounter. Spokesmen for covenant theology affirm the reality of divine-human encounter within the context of the community of faith. They resist in their Mennonite brother the possibility of substituting individual authority for the authority of the Holy Spirit as he is known in the church. Both positions are valid when they are understood as correctives of idolatrous forms of religious devotion. As a matter of historical fact, the Mennonites and other free-church denominations have taken very seriously the role of the community of faith through the mutual care of souls within the church. They continue in most instances to nourish the church as a fellowship of believers (*Gemeinde*) in contrast to an organization of believers (*Kirche*).[4]

[4] Wayne E. Oates, *Protestant Pastoral Counseling* (Philadelphia: The Westminster Press, 1962), p. 47.

The Context of Pastoral Counseling

The problem of how to be a disciplined member of a particular community of faith and to give ultimate obedience to God alone is acute when the community of faith is a community in name only. Max Thurian in his study, *Confession*, focuses the problem by stating the ideal:

> The communion of saints means . . . that beyond appearances . . . there exists in the parish or in the Christian community an ontological and vital relationship between those whom God has called to be saints. . . . The communion of saints is a life-stream circulated by the Holy Spirit through the members of Christ's Body. . . . To listen together to God's Word, to recite the same Creed, to receive the eucharistic bread and wine, is to enter into a mysterious but real communion.[5]

Thurian goes on to observe that the Communion table ought to extend our range of community across all barriers. Ironically the Communion table is *the* barrier across which even the most zealous ecumenical churchmen cannot cross today.

Thurian's prescription for this contradiction is twofold: (1) formation of smaller parishes in which the ideal of fellowship can be more easily realized, and (2) the mutual sharing of problems and sins with one another in the presence of a spiritual director.[6]

After exploring briefly the potential contribution of spiritual directors to the development of genuine community, Thurian retreats from the idea. He is afraid that pastors will resort either to psychological analysis or to the imposition of theological and moral points of view. He correctly judges that such pastoral techniques block the free activity of the Holy Spirit. Unfortunately, he appears not to recognize that pastoral counseling, as defined in this series of books, exists. The only alternative that Thurian can find is a recovery within Protestantism of confession in its traditional form. He seems unaware that, in urging return to the confessional, he is inviting religious privatism and spiritual isolation to renew its grip on

[5] Max Thurian, *Confession*, Studies in Ministry and Worship Series, ed. G. W. H. Lampe (London: SCM Press, Ltd., 1953), pp. 65–66.
[6] *Ibid.*, p. 69.

Protestantism. In the search for an ideal communion of saints, he risks undermining the real possibilities which exist for creation of a community of faith through small groups devoted to mutual confession of sins and the sharing of one another's burdens.[7]

Other alternatives are available for resolving the contradictions between the church as a community of faith and pastoral counseling as a private relationship between pastor and parishioner (either as an individual or in groups). Increasingly, pastoral counselors are admitting the reality of the contradiction, and this in itself is a step toward its resolution. Oates forthrightly says, "the church *is* the counselor."[8] He calls attention to the significance of financial and administrative structures in shaping the character of pastoral counseling. When the pastor's services are paid for not by the individuals served but by the church, the pastor more clearly symbolizes "the corporate good will of the church toward the individuals to whom he ministers."[9] When specialists in pastoral counseling are administratively responsible to the church in some official manner, they personally are less prone to drift away from a churchly identity. The representative character of their ministry may be more apparent to their clientele. Pastoral counseling centers and the ordained therapists who constitute the majority of those who staff them may be expected in the near future to seek closer administrative ties with the church in its institutionalized forms. No amount or kind of administrative tinkering with pastoral counseling as a subspecialty of the ministry can overcome entirely the contradiction inherent in the demands of Christian community, however.

The context of pastoral counseling is significant both for the psychotherapeutic and for the theological meaning of the conseling process. Hiltner and Colston have established the hypothesis that "people seeking counseling help from a pastor (in a church context), when other conditions are approximately equal, will tend to progress slightly further and faster in the same amount of time than they will in another setting, like that of a university counseling center."[10] They define a churchly context in terms of four factors: (1) the use of a church edifice for the setting of counseling; (2) perception of

[7] *Ibid.*, pp. 72–73.
[8] Oates, *Protestant Pastoral Counseling*, p. 117.
[9] *Ibid.*, p. 118.
[10] Seward Hiltner and Lowell G. Colston, *The Context of Pastoral Counseling* (Nashville: Abingdon Press, 1961), p. 21.

the counselor as a clergyman by the clients; (3) the counseling relationship emerging out of a generalized pastor-parishioner relationship that precedes and follows the formal counseling process; and (4) a pastoral counselor who is clear as to the ultimate, theological aim of counseling and who accepts the limitations on counseling imposed by other pastoral duties.

Colston's counseling in the Bryn Mawr Community Church in Chicago fulfills these criteria for a churchly context. In this example, pastoral counseling is structurally integral to a particular congregation. The administrative adjustments which Oates calls for are represented in this research design. Colston, who is a highly trained psychotherapist and also an ordained clergyman, found that for him a churchly context facilitated the achievement of the psychotherapeutic goals of counseling. These findings are validated by techniques of measurement that are consistent with contemporary canons of personality science. Pastoral counselors must come to terms with this piece of research. The psychotherapeutic goals of pastoral counseling are served best in the context of a community of faith.

What about the theological goals of pastoral counseling? The theological goals are served in part by enhancing the psychotherapeutic value of the counseling relationship. But does the counseling which Hiltner and Colston report prepare the way for disciplined dedication to a community of faith? Does pastoral counseling conducted in private pastor-parishioner relationships nurture the life of the church as a community? Is it not true that even when pastoral counseling is set within the administrative context of a particular congregation, it yields only the previously discussed indirect benefits for the life of the community?

The contradiction between the corporate nature of the church and the private, individualistic nature of pastoral counseling is partially resolved in group counseling when group counseling is conducted in the context of particular congregations. The Counseling Service of the Institute of Religion in Houston, Texas, has conducted group counseling for several years in an effort to equip ministers for group leadership in their congregations. Dr. Joseph W. Knowles, who developed the group counseling program, believes that these groups can be transplanted, with certain provisions, from their present context in an educational institution into local churches. The purpose of the groups should be clearly interpreted to and accepted by the leadership of the church, and the counseling group leader should be a minister of the congregation and should be adequately trained for the healing ministry of the church.[11]

An example of the way in which group counseling serves both individual health goals and the corporate health of a church is that of a woman who spent one year in a counseling group. She came into the group encapsulated against life and using hypochondriacal mechanisms of avoidance as her chief defense. She was excessively dependent upon her family and at the same time hostile toward family members. She was emotionally unfaithful to her husband but reacted to this by placing him upon a pedestal and worshiping him. She was irresponsibly related to her church—using her ill health and numerous operations as her excuse for remaining uninvolved. After several months in group counseling, she went through another surgical procedure. Significant change was noted. She was free of the ruminative, depressive attitudes which marked previous experiences. The surgical procedures did not whip her down this time. She also experienced a change in attitude toward her husband. Each gained freedom to communicate honestly with the other. The husband, incidentally, was a member of a different counseling group during this time. In the process she took her husband off the pedestal, and he liked it.

Then changes began to occur in relation to her larger family—the church. She began to go to people against whom she had nourished deep resentments. She opened herself to them and shared her feelings in emotionally honest ways. She discovered that they were not as exploitative and powerful as she had thought. Both she and some of those with whom she had been reconciled became more active in the life of the church. She dared to commit herself to responsibility in the church, saying, "whether I get sick or not, I'm going to tackle this job and do what I can." She reported that her behavior stimulated others in the church family to take seriously the responsibilities that they carried in the church. Because the community of faith was not accessible to the observation of the counselor, it is not possible to substantiate her reports entirely. It is reasonable to suppose, however, that had all of the members of this counseling

[11] Joseph W. Knowles, *Group Counseling* (Englewood Cliffs, N.J.: Prentice-Hall, Inc., 1964).

group been members of the same congregation, the impact of the counseling group upon the total life of the church community would have been significant.

Clearly, this woman would never have experienced freedom for genuine community with her fellow church members had she known only the content-centered study groups normally provided by churches. Before she could deal with the problems of Christian faith and life from an intellectual frame of reference, she needed to experience the wholeness and healing that comes from seeing and sharing one's own shadows. She needed to experience forgiveness and renewal within a Christian community, which in this case was the counseling group. Finally, she needed to test her new-found strength in the larger community of the church and find in a task-centered rather than a health-centered group a durable community.

I am not prepared to say that group counseling in the context of the church is *the* answer to the lack of disciplined dedication to the community of faith. I am prepared to say that group counseling prepares the way for the emergence of a sense of the corporate reality of the church. It begets trust of group processes that prepare the way for obedience to one's community of faith. The problem of how to actualize the corporate reality of the church in contemporary life is far bigger than the problems inherent in the nature of pastoral counseling. Pastoral counseling in its privatized form is a symptom, not a cause, of the absence of genuine community in the institutionalized church. It is in one sense an interim form of ministry. Pastoral counseling symbolizes the potential concern of a church that has lost its power effectively to actualize its concern for troubled people. The absence of true *koinonia* in the church calls for more serious attention to the immediate task of equipping ministers for counseling as a representative ministry of the whole church. It calls for more imaginative developments within the counseling movement—such as the group counseling mentioned above. Ultimately, it calls for the equipping of ministers not only as counselors but also as "equippers" or training supervisors of the laity. The minister would become a true "teaching elder" were he equipped for the equipping of the laity for pastoral ministry. Only when entire congregations accept corporate responsibility for shepherding, and only when laymen, as well as ministers, are adequately prepared for counseling ministries will it be possible to say that in reality "the church *is* the counselor."

What then is required for the preparation of ministers—both ordained and lay—for counseling? How shall leadership be equipped for the actualization of the church as the shepherd? The clinical education of clergymen for pastoral care and counseling now has a 40-year history in preparing clergymen as shepherds. In this history, as in other developments of recent decades, I believe that Jesus Christ, the Good Shepherd, is taking on new form. Our remaining task is to carefully examine this history for clues as to the elements essential not only in equipping individual clergymen but also in equipping churches for a corporate ministry of shepherding and healing.

CHAPTER NINE

PREPARE The WAY For A COMMUNITY
Of LEARNING And MINISTRY

Theology and pastoral counseling do not truly meet until theologians and pastoral counselors encounter one another as persons. Theologians and pastoral counselors do not exist in a social vacuum. Each is formed by a community of learning marked by its own initiation rites, rituals and jargon. Each is tempted to feel that his own discipline is self-sufficient, yet each longs for a widened and deepened community of learning and of ministry. Each exists ultimately for the sake of the church as a community of worship and of ministry to the world. It is in relation to the community of faith in its concrete, organized life that theology and pastoral counseling interpenetrate most completely.

The relationship between theology and pastoral counseling involves two factors: (1) the relationship between the communities of learning devoted to each discipline, and (2) the relationship of both to the church. The worth of this or any study of theology and pastoral functioning is its ability to facilitate communication between the two communities of learning and to prepare the way for a community of worship in which God may more wholeheartedly be glorified and enjoyed.

For centuries theology has been nourished in communities of scholars. Today these communities are our theological seminaries. Pastoral counseling is a new field not quite half a century old, if one measures its life in relation to the clinical pastoral education of ministers. Pastoral counseling has been nourished in communities of healers—chaplains, physicians, nurses, social workers, psychologists, penologists and the like. These communities center in our hospitals, social agencies, prisons, and rehabilitation and counseling centers. *The problem of relating theology and pastoral counseling is fundamentally the problem of bringing these two communities into real, dialogical relationship with each other in the context of the ministry of the church.* A review of their relationship during the past 40 years shows some consistent trends.

Campus and Clinical Communities of Theological Learning

Early efforts to form communities of learning and ministry, in which theologians and physicians joined in the training of ministers, occurred in clinical communities apart from seminary campuses. Leaders felt that new wine skins were needed, that is, new educational structures, if the educational ferment involved in becoming effective shepherds and healers were to occur. The first clinical community devoted to equipping ministers for pastoral care and counseling was formed by the interaction of The Very Rev. Samuel A. B. Mercer, Dean of Bexley Hall, and Dr. William S. Keller, M.D. In the summer of 1923, Dr. Keller housed five Bexley Hall seminarians in his home and arranged for their employment in various social agencies of Cincinnati, Ohio. Days were spent in direct service to troubled people through the social agencies; evenings were spent with Dr. Keller in his home reporting on the day's events and evaluating their experiences. Weekends afforded opportunities for ministry in various parishes and missions.

In 1927 the Bexley Hall Plan was reorganized as the "Summer School in Social Service for Theological Students and Junior Clergy." A clergyman, The Rev. Gilbert P. Symonds, joined Dr. Keller in the supervision of eight seminarians who attended. The educational formula of dual supervision by a theologian and physician was successful. In 1936 the Summer School became a year-round program called the Graduate School of Applied Religion and Dr. Joseph F. Fletcher became Dean. Clinical work was concentrated in Cincinnati's Family Society, where students working as social case workers carried small case loads under social work supervision. Classwork was as important as clinical work, however. Fletcher sought to discover "the apologetic witness" of clinical experience. A rigorous schedule of seminars was devoted to the task of correlation between the scientific and the theological perspectives.

The Graduate School closed during World War II for lack of students. It had demonstrated the value to ministers of a community of learning built on the partnership of pastoral and professional workers in the behavioral sciences. It pointed, also, to the need for a true internship for ministers—as against mere apprenticeship. True internship requires full-time study in clinical and classroom settings for at least a year. A great deal of subsequent experience confirms the findings of these early educational experimenters. Readiness for effective ministry among troubled persons usually requires at least one post-graduate year of theological education in clinical settings under expert supervision.

Better known than Keller's work is that of the Rev. Anton T. Boisen. After recovering from an emotional illness, Boisen became chaplain of the Worcester (Massachusetts) State Hospital. Richard C. Cabot, M.D., who had been Boisen's friend and teacher in the graduate school of Harvard, helped him to secure the chaplaincy position. In the fall of 1924, Cabot began teaching a course in the pastoral care of troubled persons to senior seminarians at the Episcopal Theological Seminary at Cambridge. During the Christmas recess he sent several students to Worcester State Hospital to talk with Boisen about employment there the following summer. Boisen says that this visit gave him the idea which flowered into clinical training for theological students in mental hospitals. In the summer of 1925, Boisen created a community of learning and ministry in the hospital in which he, as a theologian, and psychiatrists on the hospital staff became partners in the education of ministers.

Just as plans for the summer program were taking shape, Boisen was designated Lecturer and Research Associate in the Social Ethics Department of Chicago Theological Seminary. He spent one quarter in residence annually until 1932 when he moved to Elgin State Hospital in the Chicago area. (Boisen was succeeded as chaplain supervisor at Worcester by one of his students, Dr. Carroll A. Wise.) Immediately Boisen organized a Chicago Council for Clinical Training, on which served a number of theological educators. He continued to teach in Chicago Theological Seminary and to offer training to seminarians within the hospital. Boisen saw the seminarians' hospital experience as "theological education—via the clinic."[1]

Keller and Boisen created communities of learning and ministry in which theologians and behavioral scientists met in the equipping

[1] Anton T. Boisen, "Theological Education—Via the Clinic," *Religious Education*, March, 1930, p. 5.

of ministers. Both in Cincinnati and in Chicago, however, these interdisciplinary communities were formed in the health and welfare institutions primarily; they were not in the main stream of theological education. Andover-Newton Theological School of Boston first created a professorship in this new field and made a serious effort to incorporate an interprofessional community into its campus community of learning.

The Reverend Philip Guiles played a leading role in the organization of the Council for the Clinical Training of Theological Students in Boston in 1930. Guiles was a member of Boisen's class of 1928. By 1932 he was a full-time professor in Andover-Newton with the title, "Director of Clinical Training." The following year the Reverend Russell L. Dicks became chaplain of Massachusetts General Hospital and field secretary of the Council. Both ministers were endorsed by Cabot, who had continued to be active in the development of clinical education for ministers. Dicks and Guiles soon joined forces and began to build another community of theological learning and pastoral ministry.

In 1934 Cabot retired from Harvard's chair of Social Ethics and became Professor of Sociology and Applied Christianity in Andover-Newton. Here Cabot and Guiles had the opportunity to actualize a dream that Cabot had first announced in 1925. Cabot said that effective education for parish work requires a year of clinical study. More important, the seminary itself should become a community of both learning and of ministry. Cabot speaks for himself in the following passage:

They should have (as medical students have) a chance to watch their teachers doing the thing that they (the students) need to learn: talking with patients, tackling difficult personal problems and often failing. Medical students see their teachers grapple with a difficult medical problem and often fail to solve it or make a mess of it. This is good both for teachers and for students. They see their teacher's patience, his courage, his ingenuity, his tact tried, hard pressed, struggling, sometimes splendidly successful, sometimes a flat failure. Medical students see all this. Theological students will see it when their teachers take . . . one of their proper places in the difficult wrestle of personal relations. Their labors in another of their proper places—in the theological seminary, its lecture rooms and chapel—will then be multiplied many times in value. For, with the experiences of the hospital, the asylum, the almshouse, *held in common memory by students and teachers, who have faced them together,* the lecture, the sermon, the prayer will be enormously enhanced in educative power.[2]

Other men than Cabot dreamed the dream of a community in which pastoral ministry would serve theological learning throughout a seminary curriculum. The vitality of the idea is nowhere more evident than in a bold and creative experiment in the Protestant Episcopal Divinity School in Philadelphia. In 1935 Dean Allan Evans conferred with Helen Flanders Dunbar, M.D., The Reverend Seward Hiltner of the Council for the Clinical Training of Theological Students and The Reverend Reuel L. Howe. They emerged in 1937 with "The New Plan of Theological Education." Howe became professor of pastoral theology with three faculty associates. Howe's associates were Robert Morris and Ernest E. Bruder, who supervised clinical training in a general and mental hospital respectively, and Robert N. Stretch, who supervised senior seminarians in parish work. Students engaged in one quarter of full-time clinical training in each of the three settings, receiving a total of three quarters of training during their 3-year course of study. The New Plan was creative in design and daring in execution. It went beyond anything done even in the Boston area toward the integration of clinical training into the theological curriculum. Yet the New Plan was bitterly opposed. When Reuel Howe accepted a similar position at Virginia Theological Seminary in 1944, the New Plan was abandoned by the Philadelphia Divinity School.

The Philadelphia experiment failed largely because of the suspicions and misunderstandings of the faculty members not directly involved. Only one member of the faculty not engaged in the clinical teaching is known ever to have visited any of the training centers. Howe says, "Even though we were trying to integrate clinical training into the theological curriculum, it appeared that we were corrupting the training of men for the ministry." He adds a confession: "I contributed to its deterioration by being too impatient and too defensive."[3] Objective problems were also involved, inasmuch as the academic qualifications of Howe's associates were not of the conventional sort. Fundamentally, the New Plan failed

2 Richard C. Cabot, M.D., *Adventures on the Borderlands of Ethics* (New York: Harper & Row, Publishers, 1926), p. 10.
3 Personal communication with Dr. Reuel L. Howe.

because the entire seminary community was neither committed to nor participant in a community of both learning and ministry. Clinical training for pastoral care and counseling was identified exclusively with one department of the seminary. Not until clinical settings are seen to be as relevant to the Departments of Theology and Biblical Interpretation, for example, as they are to the Department of Pastoral Care and Counseling will the Philadelphia Plan be successful.

In these early programs of clinical pastoral education we see men struggling to build communities in which theological learning and clinical pastoral ministry could interpenetrate. During the 1940's, centers such as Boston and Chicago continued to integrate theology and counseling. A segment of the clinical training movement released its grip upon theological inquiry, however, and devoted major attention to the exploration of psychotherapy as a resource for personal fulfillment and pastoral ministry. Rebellion against everything conventional and traditional accompanied this phase. Supervisors of clinical pastoral training shared a common hostility against seminaries, seminary faculties and seminary educational policies. Often they directed their hostility against the leaders of the institutional church as well. They expressed their independence in bizarre ways. In all of their defiance, however, they expressed genuine seriousness about finding a more relevant form of theological education and of pastoral ministry. We should remember that most of the leaders in clinical theological education during this period were the products of a theological education that was grossly irrelevant.

By the 1950's, leaders in clinical pastoral education were moving toward a common identity as clinical theological educators. Concern grew rapidly to incorporate training in pastoral counseling into the seminary learning of theology. Simultaneously, men in the clinical field became seekers after the theological sources of pastoral ministry. By 1956 a number of educational innovations as far-reaching as the New Plan of Theological Education were securely established. H. Richard Niebuhr and associates published a comprehensive study of theological education at this time. The emergence of communities in which theological learning and pastoral ministry are integrated is wholeheartedly endorsed in the Niebuhr study.[4]

[4] H. Richard Niebuhr, Daniel Day Williams and James M. Gustafson, *The Advancement of Theological Education* (New York: Harper & Row,

Niebuhr justifies these educational innovations on the ground that previous theories of the relationship between reflection and action are inadequate. Clinical work is indispensable to theological learning because it saves theological education from the illusion that rational comprehension is adequate alone. Theological education is not simply the attaining of "intellectual comprehension." It is also a process of nurturing students "into the measure of the stature of the fullness of Christ."[5] On the basis of this educational principle, Niebuhr and his associates affirm that the new emphasis in psychology and pastoral counseling represents "a significant new turn in the education of the ministry."[6]

Theology and Pastoral Counseling in the Church

We have come full circle. Initially, theology makes a demand of pastoral ministry. Theology confronts pastoral care and counseling with its neglect of the doctrine of the church as the shepherd. Now the church confronts the theological community with a demand for the preparation of ministers with unusual qualifications. The ultimate test of theological education is the quality of lay learning, lay shepherding and lay witnessing that occurs in the churches, or through the churches in the world. The ministerial leadership needed to implement the ideal of the church as shepherd must be more psychologically and sociologically sophisticated than ever before. A minister must be secure enough to be open to dialogue. He must be prepared for divine-human encounter in the midst of human relationships. He must be equipped to prepare the way for others to be encountered by God, particularly those in psychic and social pain and suffering. His theological learning must be integrated into his pastoral ministry; he must enjoy a large measure of unification between head and heart. He must be free to mobilize

Publishers, 1956), pp. 125–126: Two examples of the integration of a theological community of learning and a clinical community of ministry are mentioned. They are the Southern Baptist Theological Seminary in Louisville, Kentucky, and the Institute of Religion in the Texas Medical Center, Houston, Texas.

[5] H. Richard Niebuhr, *The Purpose of the Church and Its Ministry: Reflections on the Aims of Theological Education* (New York: Harper & Row, Publishers, 1956), pp. 126, 132–133.

[6] Niebuhr, *The Advancement of Theological Education*, pp. 128–129.

his own person in ministry. He must find fulfillment not in star-dom but in coaching, not in ruling but in teaching, not in perform-ing as the religious expert but in equipping the laity for ministry in every cell of the social organism.

In these pages I have said that theology and pastoral counseling interpenetrate. They interpenetrate in ministry and in learning. I have described this interpenetration in my own experience and in the ministry of others. I believe, finally, that theology and pastoral counseling interpenetrate in mutual fulfillment in the church. Pas-toral counseling will fulfill its potential as it takes more seriously its function as a representative of the church and as it serves the church through the formation of a corporate community of healing and of witnessing. Theology will fulfill its potential as it re-forms the structures of seminary education to be a representative of the church—to be a community of faith. As theological inquiry extends the dialogue with clinical pastoral ministry, it participates in the preparation of men for faith as well as for professional functioning. It equips ministers not only as scholars but also as persons free to enter into dialogue with themselves and their congregations—and corporately with the world. Theology finds itself fulfilled as it is formed and re-formed in ministry, while pastoral ministry, especially pastoral counseling, finds itself fulfilled as it is formed and re-formed by theology.

I hope it is now clear that a minister who takes pastoral care and counseling seriously need not cut himself off from theological in-quiry. A theologian need not live on the balcony of life in order to pursue his task. Pastoral care and counseling is both a method of communicating theology and a means of understanding it. Theology forms both the theory and the practice of pastoral ministries.

When theology and pastoral counseling meet, notable results occur. Theological education is transformed as it sustains the di-alogue between theology and pastoral counseling. Individual min-isters find in theological education of this kind significant help in the unification of the theology one believes with the theology that irrationally shapes the way one behaves. But, to me, the most compelling reason for involvement in the dialogue between theology and pastoral counseling is *the hope that in the dialogue the church will be enabled more fully to "prepare the way of the Lord."* The interpenetration of theology and pastoral counseling fulfills in part,

at least, the hope of Isaiah, which was also the hope of the early
Christian community:

> Every valley shall be filled,
> and every mountain and hill shall be brought low,
> and the crooked shall be made straight,
> and the rough ways shall be made smooth;
> and all flesh shall see the salvation of God (Luke 3:4–6).

BIBLIOGRAPHY

Books

BOISEN, ANTON T., *The Exploration of the Inner World, A Study of Mental Disorder and Religious Experience.* New York: Willett, Clark and Company, 1936.

BONHOEFFER, DIETRICH, *Ethics.* New York: The Macmillan Company, 1955.

BRETALL, ROBERT, ed., *A Kierkegaard Anthology.* Princeton: Princeton University Press, 1951.

BRUNNER, EMIL, *Justice and the Social Order.* New York: Harper & Row, Publishers, 1945.

CABOT, RICHARD C., M.D., *Adventures on the Border Lands of Ethics.* New York: Harper & Row, Publishers, 1926.

DICKS, RUSSELL L., *How to Make Pastoral Calls: A Guidebook in Pastoral Calling for Ministers and Laymen.* St. Louis: The Bethany Press, 1962.

DONIGER, SIMON, ed., *The Nature of Man: In Theological and Psychological Perspective.* New York: Harper & Row, Publishers, 1962.

HILTNER, SEWARD and LOWELL G. COLSTON, *The Context of Pastoral Counseling.* Nashville: Abingdon Press, 1961.

JUNG, CARL G., *The Development of Personality,* Vol. 17, translated by R. F. C. Hull, Bollingen Series XX. New York: Pantheon Books, 1953.

JUNG, CARL G., *Psychology and Alchemy,* Vol. 12, Bollingen Series XX. New York: Pantheon Books, 1953.

KNOWLES, JOSEPH W., *Group Counseling.* Englewood Cliffs, N.J.: Prentice-Hall, Inc., 1964.

MAEDER, ALPHONSE, *Ways to Psychic Health.* New York: Charles Scribner's Sons, 1953.

NIEBUHR, H. RICHARD, *The Meaning of Revelation.* New York: The Macmillan Company, 1962.

NIEBUHR, H. RICHARD, *The Purpose of the Church and Its Ministry: Reflections on the Aims of Theological Education.* New York: Harper & Row, Publishers, 1956.

NIEBUHR, H. RICHARD, DANIEL DAY WILLIAMS and JAMES M. GUSTAFson, *The Advancement of Theological Education*. New York: Harper & Row, Publishers, 1956.

OATES, WAYNE E., *Christ and Selfhood*. New York: Association Press, 1961.

OATES, WAYNE E., *Protestant Pastoral Counseling*. Philadelphia: The Westminster Press, 1962.

PUSSEY, EDWARD B., trans., *The Confessions of Saint Augustine*. New York: The Modern Library, 1949.

ROBERTS, DAVID E., *Psychotherapy and the Christian View of Man*. New York: Charles Scribner's Sons, 1951.

The Interpreter's Bible, IX, Nashville, Abingdon-Cokesbury Press, 1951.

THURIAN, MAX, *Confession*, Studies in Ministry and Worship Series, ed. by G. W. H. Lampe. London: SCM Press, Ltd., 1953.

THURNEYSEN, EDUARD, *A Theology of Pastoral Care*. Richmond, Va.: John Knox Press, 1962.

TILLICH, PAUL, *Love, Power and Justice*. New York: Oxford University Press, 1954; Gloucester, Mass.: Peter Smith, 1960.

TILLICH, PAUL, *The Courage To Be*. New Haven: Yale University Press, 1952.

TOURNIER, PAUL, *A Doctor's Casebook in the Light of the Bible*, translated by Edwin Hudson. New York: Harper & Row, Publishers, 1960.

WISE, CARROLL A., *Religion in Illness and Health*. New York: Harper & Row, Publishers, 1942.

Articles and Dissertations

GAYLE, R. FINLEY, JR., M.D., "Conflict and Cooperation Between Psychiatry and Religion," *American Journal of Psychiatry*, XIII, July, 1956, pp. 1–7.

LAPSLEY, JAMES N., JR., "Pastoral Counseling Centers: Mid-Century Phenomenon," *Pastoral Psychology*, XIII, No. 130 (1963), pp. 43–52.

THORNTON, EDWARD E., "These Deacons Led Out," *Church Administration*, I, No. 3 (1959), pp. 34–35.

THORNTON, EDWARD E., "A Critique of Clinical Pastoral Education," Unpublished Doctoral Dissertation, Southern Baptist Theological Seminary, Louisville, Ky., June, 1961.

WALTER, ORVILLE S., "Metaphysics, Religion, and Psychotherapy," *Journal of Counseling Psychology*, V, No. 4 (1958), pp. 243–252.

WORTHINGTON, JACK A., "Anxiety and Forgiveness in Pastoral Care: A Critical and Constructive Study of the Adequacy of Eduard Thurneysen's Theology of Pastoral Care and Oskar Pfister's Pastoral Analysis for Facing the Parishioner's Anxiety," Unpublished Doctoral Dissertation, Divinity School of the University of Chicago, June, 1961.

INDEX

Physical handicap, 31
Possession, 105ff
Prayer, 57, 82f, 103, 116
  see: Ministry, use of Scripture
    and prayer
Preaching, 38f, 71, 97, 103
Preparation of the way, 27, 29, 32,
    34, 38ff, 56f, 67, 71, 73, 76f,
    84, 86, 89, 93f, 99f, 102,
    107, 110, 118, 123, 133ff
Prostitution, 64, 67
Protestantism, 53, 74, 121f
Psychiatry, 18ff, 35, 48f, 53, 56,
    58f, 65f, 68, 71, 93, 101f,
    105, 108ff, 121f, 132
Psychology of religion, 54
Psychosis, 30, 66

Rationality-irrationality, 86f, 94ff,
    106, 109, 117, 134
Rationalization, 88
Reassurance, 19
Rebellion, 72, 89
Recreation, 106
Redemption, 84
Referral, 21f
Reformed theology
  see: Theology, Reformed
Relationship, 85ff, 105f, 118, 120
Repentance, 67f, 70, 72, 73, 79,
    86ff
Repression, 61, 86ff, 102, 104
Resignation, 89
Resurrection, 113
Revelation, 16, 28
Riesman, 90
Roberts, David E., 93f
Roman Catholicism, 53, 74

Salvation, 20, 27f, 34, 58, 85f, 92,
    96, 119, 135
  and health, 22, 32f, 40f, 57,
    67, 69f, 72, 86, 93f, 125,
    134
Sanctification, 34, 72
Scripture, see Ministry, use of
  Scripture and prayer

Security operations, 77, 88
Selective inattention, 88f, 91, 98
Self-consistency, 80
Self-esteem, 86, 88f, 100, 106
Self-justification, 63, 67, 76, 91f
Self pity, 62
Sex, 21, 63, 65, 67, 90, 98, 106,
    109
Sharing, 72, 121
Sin, 17, 32, 35, 40, 51ff, 70, 72,
    75f, 90f, 94, 112, 119, 121
  original, 18
Speech impediment, 31
Spirits
  false, 54
  testing of, 54, 116, 118
Spontaneity, 94, 106, 113
Stretch, Robert N., 131
Suicide, 19f
Sullivan, Harry Stack, 77, 88
Sunday School, 24
Surgery, 54f, 71, 124
Symonds, Gilbert P., 128

Temptation, 39, 90, 110
Theological education, 128ff
Theology
  empirical inquiry, 16
  of suffering, 19
  Reformed, 49, 120
  relation to pastoral care, 15f,
    25f, 54, 59, 72, 73, 86f,
    90, 127, 134
Thurian, Max, 121f
Thurneysen, Eduard, 34, 48ff
Tillich, Paul, 25, 34
Tournier, Paul, M.D., 56
Transference, 68, 97

Ulcers, 33
Ultimate, 39f, 57f, 70f, 84, 92, 97,
    108, 122
Unconscious, 19, 29f, 39, 54, 61f,
    66, 68, 87f, 92f, 95, 97ff,
    102ff
Unwed mothers, 16f